S0-AXN-559

In Search of Margaret Fuller

In Search of Margaret Fuller

A Biography by
Abby Slater

DELACORTE PRESS / NEW YORK

Published by
Delacorte Press
1 Dag Hammarskjold Plaza
New York, New York 10017

Manufactured in the United States of America

First printing

Designed by MaryJane DiMassi

Library of Congress Cataloging in Publication Data

Slater, Abby.
In search of Margaret Fuller.

Bibliography: p.
SUMMARY: A biography of critic, journalist, and social reformer.
1. Ossoli, Sarah Margaret Fuller, marchesa d', 1810–1850—Biography. 2. Authors, American—19th century—Biography. [1. Ossoli, Sarah Margaret Fuller, marchesa d', 1810–1850. 2. Authors, American]
I. Title.
PS2506.S57 818'.3'09 [B] [92] 77–86335
ISBN 0–440–03944–4

for
Marilynn Meeker
who cares about
Margaret

Contents

I

The Shipwreck

In the Mount Auburn Cemetery in Cambridge, Massachusetts, is a memorial monument with these words on it:

IN MEMORY OF
MARGARET FULLER OSSOLI
BORN IN CAMBRIDGE, MASS. MAY 23, 1810

BY BIRTH A CHILD OF NEW ENGLAND
BY ADOPTION A CITIZEN OF ROME
BY GENIUS BELONGING TO THE WORLD
IN YOUTH
AN INSATIATE STUDENT, SEEKING THE HIGHEST CULTURE
IN RIPER YEARS
TEACHER, WRITER, CRITIC OF LITERATURE AND ART
IN MATURER AGE
COMPANION AND HELPER OF MANY
EARNEST REFORMER IN AMERICA AND EUROPE

AND OF HER HUSBAND
GIOVANNI ANGELO, MARQUIS OSSOLI
HE GAVE UP RANK, STATION AND HOME
FOR THE ROMAN REPUBLIC
AND FOR HIS WIFE AND CHILD

AND OF THAT CHILD
ANGELO EUGENE PHILIP OSSOLI
BORN IN RIETI, ITALY, SEPTEMBER 5, 1848
WHOSE DUST REPOSES AT THE FOOT OF THIS STONE
THEY PASSED FROM THIS LIFE TOGETHER
BY SHIPWRECK JULY 19, 1850

UNITED IN LIFE THE MERCIFUL FATHER TOOK THEM
TOGETHER AND IN DEATH THEY WERE NOT DIVIDED.

The words are a fair—and even moving—outline of the facts of Margaret Fuller's life and of her death. But they answer none of the questions that nag at anyone who knows her story more fully.

Her death, for example. Was it inevitable? Others on the same ship that brought death to the Ossolis managed to save themselves. And only a few days before she set sail on her last journey, Margaret had written, in a letter to a friend:

> I am absurdly fearful, and various omens have combined to give me a dark feeling. I am become indeed a miserable coward, for the sake of Angelino. I fear heat and cold, fear the voyage, fear biting poverty. I hope I shall not be forced to be brave for him, as I have been for myself, and that, if I succeed to rear him, he will be neither a weak nor a bad man. But I love him too much! In case of mishap, however, I shall perish with my husband and my child, and we

> may be transferred to some happier state. . . . It seems to me that my future upon earth will soon close. It may be terribly trying, but it will not be so terribly long now . . . I have a vague expectation of some crisis—I know not what. . . . My life proceeds as regularly as the fate of a Greek tragedy, and I can but accept the pages as they turn . . .

So it would seem that her death was not entirely unwelcome to her. What made her so afraid? What in her life made it such a torture? The letter shows that she adored her baby. And she was devoted to her husband, as he was to her. True, he was not the kind of man anyone—including Margaret—would have expected her to marry. They were very different in many ways. And true, they had no money: they had had to borrow to pay for their passage to America.

But Margaret was well known—indeed, famous—in her native country, and once they had arrived, she would surely have been able to earn a living. Even in her moments of greatest despair, she must have known that. Why, then, was she so willing to give up her life when she was only forty years old?

That fame of hers—it, too, raises many nagging questions. It vanished so quickly. Within a few years of her death, Margaret had been demoted from a position of importance in her own right to one in which her only importance was in the company she kept. She was a friend and colleague of many of the best-known figures of her time—Ralph Waldo Emerson, Henry David Thoreau, and Horace Greeley among them—and it was by these associations, rather than by her own work and character, that she was remembered.

But were her work and character so unimportant? Was she nothing more than a handmaiden to a group of illustrious men? She was, after all, the editor of a major magazine, the organ of expression of Transcendentalism, a movement that shocked the conventional thought of her time and opened the way for the development of a distinctively American way of looking at life and at ideas. She was the author of the first book ever published in this country on woman's rights. She was the first woman ever to be employed as a critic and journalist on the staff of a daily newspaper. She was the first American journalist ever to serve as a foreign correspondent. She was, in other words, a pioneer—a member of a breed Americans have always celebrated.

And why, in her own time, was fame accorded to her so grudgingly? Why were so many people so critical of her? The reason for some of the criticism is clear. Many of Margaret's ideas were revolutionary and, therefore, unpopular—her advocacy of full equality for women, for example. At a time when women were not supposed to work unless they had to, and then were supposed to follow the "feminine" vocations—as seamstresses, or teachers, or writers on "feminine" subjects—Margaret proposed that women could, and should, do anything they felt called to do. "If you ask me what office women should fill," she wrote, "I reply—any . . . let them be sea captains, if you will. I do not doubt that there are women well fitted for such an office."

But the criticisms of Margaret went far beyond criticism of her ideas. She was an object of caricature and malice, someone to be laughed about behind her back—not only by those who hated the ideas she stood for, but even by her allies and friends. It was almost obligatory to make fun of Margaret, to sneer at her looks and at her manners, and to gossip about her personal life. What was there about the woman that aroused in other people the impulse to be mean?

It cannot have been envy. Margaret's life was far from enviable. Her childhood was difficult and painful, and its nightmares—both the ones that woke her, sobbing, from her bed and the ones that formed her daily life—inevitably left their mark on her. Only a fairyland life as an adult could have erased the misery of her years of growing up. And such an adult life she did not have. Was the shipwreck the last intolerable obstacle—an obstacle she no longer had the energy to surmount?

There were many earlier ones. There was, for example, the obstacle of her sex. The United States in the early years of the nineteenth century was hardly likely to reward a woman who criticized it and asserted herself, and who refused to take a back seat to any man, no matter what his reputation or importance. And Margaret *was* critical and self-assertive. False modesty was never one of her sins. She had a strong sense of her own worth and her own abilities, and never pretended to be less than she was. Such self-esteem was outrageous in a woman, and even Margaret's closest male friends resented it. Emerson, who admired her enormously, wrote in a memoir published after her death that she had a "mountainous me," and went on to report a comment she once had made to him: "I now know all the people worth knowing in America, and I find no intellect comparable to my own." The remark was, of course, doubly arrogant because a woman had made it.

But if Margaret's unhappy childhood laid the groundwork for an unhappy adult life, if Margaret's sex was a constant handicap, and if Margaret's character—like everyone's—was flawed, that still does not explain the difficulties she experienced. Something more must have been at work, something that made her an easy target when she was living and that made it convenient to ignore her in the years after her death.

Perhaps it was her uncompromising idealism. Margaret was not a fool, and she certainly knew the realities of the country she lived in. But she also knew what her country *ought* to be. And the oughts that inspired Margaret were not her personal creation—they were those that had guided the nation's founders and were written into its Constitution: equality, democracy, and mutual respect. Margaret Fuller believed in a world of principle, and she believed that other people were as eager as she to bring such a world into being. Her principles were part of her character, and inseparable from it.

An idealist always makes people uneasy—especially if she is a woman. All her virtues fade beside her overriding fault: the constant reminder she presents to other people of their own failures of courage, of spirit, and of belief. It would be so much nicer—so much easier—if she would just go away. Such a person is, to put it bluntly, extremely troublesome.

But Margaret did not go away when she was living, and will not go away today, more than a hundred years later. With all her unhappiness, all her self-assertion and idealism, she is still a part of our lives.

Life is never easy for a prodigy. And Margaret was doomed to be a prodigy almost from the moment of her birth. She was born to a set of parents who would have made things difficult for any child: a talented, disappointed, domineering father and a mother ten years his junior who had been a schoolteacher before her marriage but retreated into ineffectuality once she became Mrs. Fuller. From the moment of her marriage, she abdicated all her judgment and authority to her husband, and when Margaret was born, she permitted him to take over their daughter's education and upbringing. He was parent, teacher, and disciplinarian all in one, and his wife never lifted a finger to stop him from putting relentless pressure on his oldest child.

Not that he thought he was making things difficult, or that he did not love her. On the contrary. According to his lights, he loved her deeply and he had high hopes for her. Why else would he come home after a full day's work in his law office to spend the evening teaching Latin and English grammar to a six-year-old girl? Why else would he drill her so thoroughly that, by the time she was seven, she had read all of Virgil, Horace, and Ovid? Such an advanced education was unusual even for a boy that young. It was unheard of for a girl.

No doubt, Timothy Fuller would have preferred to teach a boy. When his first child was born, he was so proud and delighted that he planted two trees in her honor at the entrance to his house. But even so, he felt a twinge of disappointment at her sex. He had always wanted his child to be his greatest accomplishment, and to find the fame and approval his own prickly personality had denied him. That meant a boy-child, obviously, and his first child was not a boy. Nor was the second. Sons were eventually born into the Fuller family—five of them. But long before their arrival Timothy Fuller had made his decision. He would raise his firstborn daughter as he would have raised a son. She would be a student and a thinker—and a child of the principles that had led Americans to revolt against the British Crown. But by the time of Margaret's birth in 1810, the Revolution was ancient history. Its gains had been won, and the new nation was set on a course of material achievement and ideological orthodoxy. It was proud of itself and impatient of criticism—and nowhere was it more complacent than in New England, with its Puritan heritage of rigidity and fear of sin. Margaret was born into a time and place that had little use for nonconformity of any sort, and no use at all for that worst of all nonconformists: a child who knew more than most adults; a girl who was far brighter and better educated than most boys.

So it is not surprising that she was a solitary and unhappy youngster and that she suffered from almost intolerable nightmares throughout her childhood. They began even before she fell asleep, when the dark around her became alive with grotesque, disembodied faces—faces that moved noiselessly toward her, grimacing horribly—and continued as dreams of horses trampling over her, of long and mournful funeral processions to a grave that turned out to be her mother's, of dense forests with trees dripping blood. Sometimes she woke up shaking and weeping and covered with sweat. Sometimes she wandered, still asleep, moaning through the house. On those occasions, when her parents found her and awakened her, she would try to tell them of her terror. But they would not listen. "Leave off thinking of such nonsense," her father would say sternly, "or you will become crazy." Which only added a new fear to the old ones and made the days nearly as awful as the nights.

But with all the nightmare terrors, there were excitements and satisfactions in Margaret's rigorous life. The world of the mind fascinated and enchanted her, and she would never have dreamed of exchanging it for the more ordinary world of other girls her age—the world of dolls and sewing and baking. Although she was often tormented by being the kind of person she was, she would have been bored and frustrated with any other life. She was torn by a constant battle: the battle between her high abilities and exalted aspirations, on the one hand, and the loneliness they brought her in a world that frowned on young girls so learned and so different on the other.

So Margaret grew up a high-strung, bookish, withdrawn, dreamy girl who spent her days, when she was not studying, either in her mother's garden or her father's library. The garden, which was her mother's joy, was a joy to Margaret also, and she turned the sweet-smelling roses and the delicate violets and lilies into models for herself, vowing to become as pure and perfect and beautiful as they. The library was a somewhat more mixed blessing. The more she read and loved the works of genius she found there, the more she despaired of her own abilities. How could she ever hope to have a mind or pen as brilliant as Shakespeare's? The more she read and loved the classics, with their dramas of nobility, intrigue, and high passion, the more stagnant and dull her everyday life seemed—Cambridge, Massachusetts was a whole universe away from Caesar's Rome.

Then, one Sunday morning at church, when she was thirteen, she met a young Englishwoman named Ellen Kilshaw, who brought all the romance and excitement of Europe to boring middle-class New England. For a while, all Margaret's dreams seemed to be coming true. Ellen was visiting in Cambridge with friends who were also friends of Margaret's family, and she soon became a regular guest at the Fuller home. She was several years older than Margaret, and everything that Margaret hoped so desperately to become. She had about her a mysterious air of elegance and reserve: the way she dressed, the way she wore her hair, the faint, sweet scent that lingered around her, the clipped and precise accent in which she spoke—all of them were exotic.

She had still more qualities that Margaret admired. She was an accomplished painter; she played beautifully on the harp; she was a devoted reader of the works of Sir Walter Scott. Moreover, she was impressed by Margaret's mind and flattered by her attention, and she made the child her protégée. She and Margaret took long walks together and spent long hours in earnest conversation.

But Ellen's visit lasted only a few months, and when she returned to England, Margaret was desolated. It seemed to her that the end of the world had come. "The light of life was set," she wrote—much later—of her feelings at that time, "and every leaf was withered," and she withdrew even further into herself, wandering disconsolately through the house or sitting silently in the shadows, refusing to talk or eat, and growing painfully thin.

Something had to be done, Timothy Fuller decided. Perhaps Margaret would be better off away from home, in the company of girls her own age. He had heard good reports of the Misses Prescott's school in Groton, forty miles from Cambridge. So Margaret was packed off there.

The first few months were pleasant. Margaret felt not one moment of homesickness. Indeed, she was glad to escape the pressure of her family. In addition, for those first few months she was extremely popular both with her schoolmates and with her teachers. The girls found her just as exotic as she had found Ellen, and they competed with one another for the honor of her friendship. The teachers were rapturous at the appearance of such a brilliant scholar in their classes. Margaret came out of her shell. She studied hard and played hard; she was happy once again.

Then things began to go sour. The first glorious impressions faded and the problems began to emerge. Margaret had never before had any friends her own age, and she had no experience in getting along with other girls. At home, Margaret was the oldest, and if she deigned to spend any time with the younger children, they looked upon it as an honor and cheerfully accepted her leadership. At school, Margaret took it for granted that the same pattern would prevail, and she ordered the girls around as if she were a queen. At first, because they found her so exciting, they willingly subordinated themselves to her. But after a while they rebelled and, resentful of her imperious ways, excluded her from their games and conversations and cliques. Margaret was now more alone than she had ever been.

The teachers, too, began to dislike her. At home, Margaret had been used to a certain pattern of daily activity. The day was for quiet: for reading and writing and walking through the garden behind the house, rehearsing to herself what she had learned. The evening was for excitement: for presenting to her father the fruits of her day's learning and enjoying his pleasure in her accomplishments. At first, the teachers accepted the change that came over their prize scholar when the sun had set; they thought it was merely a sign that she had not yet adjusted to life at school. But the behavior persisted. In the evening, after dinner, when she should have been preparing herself for bed, Margaret would spin around in circles, her skirts flying, reciting verses and acting all the characters in scenes from Shakespeare's plays; she would become so overstimulated that she could not go to sleep until long after everyone else. And when she finally crawled into bed, it was as if she had once again become a small child. Her nightmares and her sleepwalking returned. Night after night she wandered through the halls, frightening any of the girls who happened to catch sight of her ghostly figure.

The warfare between Margaret and the rest of the school simmered for months and finally burst into the open. Margaret had the notion that she looked prettier when she had high color, and she regularly used the rouge the other girls wore only in school theatricals, painting an obvious pink blush on her cheeks every morning. One evening she entered the dining room, late, for dinner. She always disliked the mealtime ceremonial, with everyone sitting quietly at long tables, waiting—almost in silence—to be served, and she always postponed her arrival as long as she could. As she took her seat, she noticed that the girl to her right had rouge circles on her cheeks. So did the girl to her left. As Margaret looked around, she saw that every girl in the school had rouged cheeks. The entire student body had joined in a plot to humiliate her.

Margaret said nothing. She sat silently at the table and picked at her food. None of the noble Romans or Britons she so admired would have shown any signs of their humiliation publicly, and neither would she.

But the hurt was almost unbearable, and after dinner, when she returned to her room, she locked the door, threw herself on the floor, and screamed in a tantrum of rage and shame. And she vowed revenge on her tormentors—a revenge intricate, clever, and complete enough to satisfy a Hamlet or a Marc Antony.

She became a tale-teller. She exaggerated and falsified whatever confidences came her way, and when she had no little cache of stories to distort and pass on, she invented them. Within a few weeks, she had turned the entire school into a hotbed of factions and feuds. Girls who had been best friends no longer spoke to one another. Girls who were usually cheerful and smiling looked around suspiciously, with narrowed eyes. Only Margaret, in that wilderness of misery and mistrust, was calm and unperturbed.

That calm proved her undoing. The more observant girls noticed it and began to put the pieces together and to compare experiences, until finally they figured out precisely what must have happened. Eight of them went in a body to the headmistress and told her what they had discovered. Their evidence was convincing, and Margaret was called in to defend herself.

At first, she did—with high eloquence and even higher moral indignation. How dare they accuse her of spreading tales? How dare they suggest that she would engage in conduct as petty and malicious as that? How dare they believe, even for an instant, that she, Sarah Margaret Fuller, would sink so shamefully low?

But the truth was on their side, and Margaret

knew it. Even as she spoke, every defense of herself became a self-indictment; every self-righteous outburst became a demonstration of her own hypocrisy. Her Puritan conscience rose up and smote her. She had not been a Marc Antony or a Hamlet. She had been an Iago, vengeful and malevolent.

This time when she threw herself on the floor, it was not in a tantrum. It was in a convulsion of agony, shame, and remorse. The headmistress and the girls were terrified by this passionate outburst of conscience, and they began to feel pity for Margaret, who was now punishing herself far more than she had ever punished them. But even though they forgave her, she could not forgive herself, and for weeks she was sick and silent, so overwhelmed by shame that she began to brood on suicide. "Too late," she wrote in her journal, "sin is revealed to me in all its deformity, and sin-defiled, I will not, cannot live. The mainspring of life is broken."

It took Susan Prescott, one of the owners of the school, to bring her back to her senses, and to enable her to view herself with some understanding and charity. Miss Prescott had been Margaret's ideal from the time she first came to the school, replacing Ellen Kilshaw as Margaret's model of taste and delicacy. If this collection of virtues could have risen above the early wickedness she now blushingly confessed to her pupil, Margaret felt there was hope for her, too.

2
Prodigy and Puritan

Gradually, Margaret recovered from her self-hatred and her suicidal despair. But she was still unhappy, and her father believed she would be better off in Cambridge, where he could keep an eye on her. So, when she was fifteen, he withdrew her from the Misses Prescott's school and brought her back home. Once she arrived there, she set out a program of daily activities for herself that she described in a letter to Susan Prescott.

> I rise a little before five, wait an hour and then practice on the piano until seven, when we breakfast. Next I read French—Sismondi's Literature of the South of Europe—till eight, then two or three lectures in Brown's philosophy.

> About half past nine I go to Mr. Perkins' school and study Greek until twelve when, the school being dismissed, I recite, go home and practice again until dinner, at two. Sometimes, if the conversation is very agreeable, I lounge for half an hour over the dessert, though rarely so lavish of time. Then, when I can, I read two hours in Italian, but I am often interrupted. At six, I walk or take a drive. Before going to bed I play or sing for half an hour, to make all sleepy, and about eleven, retire to write a while in my journal. . . . Thus, you can see, I am learning Greek, and making acquaintance with metaphysics, and French and Italian literature.

That was Margaret—prodigy and Puritan. The prodigy stuffed her head with knowledge like a housewife stuffing a Christmas goose; the Puritan dismissed all the joy and excitement she felt in learning, and reduced the whole experience to an exercise in conscience and responsibility. The effect was to give a kind of driven quality to almost everything she did. It was as if, in her teens, Margaret was still running from the stampeding horses that had haunted her childhood nightmares.

This strange, almost frightening intensity was very much in evidence one summer night in 1826. It was an important occasion for the entire Fuller family. President John Quincy Adams was planning to pass through Boston, and he had accepted an invitation from Margaret's father to a dinner and ball in his honor at the Fuller home. It was the first time any president had agreed to visit a private home in Boston, and Timothy Fuller was understandably proud. He decided to wring every possible piece of glory out of the evening by using it to introduce Margaret, who had just turned sixteen, to Boston society. All of its most glittering lights would, after all, be present at the ball.

Margaret was ecstatic. She wore an elaborate pink silk dress, especially made for the occasion, and she danced to every single tune the musicians played. But despite her high color and her eager exhilaration, despite her blond hair, large eyes, white teeth, and long, slender neck, few of the guests thought her pretty. Margaret was nearsighted and her gestures were clumsy. She blinked, squinted, and peered —thrusting her head forward awkwardly in order to see better. She was keyed up, overexcited—almost frantic—and long before the evening was over, her dress was wet with perspiration, and her carefully arranged curls were falling limply over her shoulders.

To make matters worse, she had few of the social graces that all properly brought-up young women were supposed to have learned at their mothers' knees. Margaret's mother, after all, had very little to do with her daughter's upbringing. Margaret was her father's daughter—a New England version of the Roman goddess of wisdom, Minerva, who, so the myth says, sprang full grown from the forehead of her father, the supreme god, Jupiter. It was bad enough, in the eyes of many Bostonians, that Margaret had what they called "a man's mind." It was even worse that she had what they regarded as a man's manner—that she displayed little of the restraint and deference every well-bred young woman was supposed to have. So it is not surprising that most of the guests at Timothy Fuller's party felt uncomfortable in her presence, and found her arrogant and unattractive.

Margaret was well aware of this. "From a very early age," she once wrote to a friend, "I have felt that I was not born to the common womanly lot. I knew that I should never find a being who could keep the key to my character, that there would be none on whom I could always lean; that I should be a pilgrim and sojourner on the earth, and that the birds and foxes would be surer of a place to lay the head than I. . . ."

But despite this gloomy picture of herself and her life, Margaret was not really lonely in Cambridge. Conventional Bostonians might be offended by her brilliance and her self-assertiveness, but Boston had its independent spirits, too, and they were fascinated and enchanted by everything about Margaret. One of her warmest admirers was Eliza Farrar, the wife of a professor at Harvard and the author of a popular book on feminine etiquette, the very area in which Margaret was most deficient. As soon as she met Margaret, Mrs. Farrar set out to rub off the sharp corners in her manner that so distressed the conventional world. Margaret was delighted to put herself in Eliza's hands. She knew that things were not likely to be easy for her, and she blamed herself for it. "I am wanting in that intuitive tact and polish which nature has bestowed on some," she wrote. She could be even more self-critical, describing herself at nineteen as "the most intolerable girl that ever took a seat in a drawing room." But though Margaret worked hard with Eliza, the training was only partially successful. Her temperament and her upbringing made her an unsuitable candidate for easy acceptability.

In addition to Eliza, Margaret's friends included many of the young women who had attended Mr. Perkins' school with her. They were fascinated by her mannerisms and her clothing, and awed by her brilliance. They hoped so much it would rub off on them that they even began to carry themselves as she did—necks pressed forward and eyes half-shut, peering intently and nearsightedly at the world. "We thought," wrote one of them, "that if we could only come into school that way, we could know as much Greek as she did."

And there were the young men, members of the Harvard class of 1829, who were excited by the new ideas that were percolating through the worlds of literature and philosophy and were delighted to find in Margaret a companion with whom they could share their discoveries and ideas. To all these people, Margaret was a heroine. And she, warmed by their admiration and affection, lived up to their highest expectations. In their company she was vivacious, not frantic; patient, not brusque; sympathetic, not arrogant.

Margaret had a special gift for friendship. Perhaps it had developed out of her unhappy experience at the Misses Prescott's school, or perhaps out of a need that was never met in her childhood—the need for a mother on whom she could depend for loving help. In her friendships, Margaret was always a strong, supportive guide, playing the role her mother never played for her. She could be, and frequently was, extremely critical; but she was never malicious. Her friends felt absolutely safe in confiding in her. They knew she would respect their secrets, and would keep them.

There were only two conditions to Margaret's friendship. She must be allowed her privacy. She wanted her friends to confide in her, but they must not ask her to confide in them. And they must aspire to elevated ideals. As she once wrote to one of her brothers, "Great and even *fatal* errors (so far as this life is concerned) could not destroy my friendship for one in whom I am sure of the kernel of nobleness." And when she detected that kernel, she was so eager to offer her friendship that her offer was bound, in time, to be accepted. "She saw when anyone belonged to her," wrote one of her friends, "and never rested until she came into possession of her property."

The man who wrote this was one of the few among Margaret's friends who was able to resist her demand for dominance in their relationship. His name was James Freeman Clarke, and he was a distant relative of Margaret's who belonged to the Harvard class of 1829. He and Margaret called each other cousin, and saw each other nearly every day, taking long walks together, or riding horseback across the countryside, always talking, talking, talking. Clarke described Margaret's gift for friendship this way:

> Margaret was, to persons younger than herself . . . wisdom and intellectual beauty, filling life with charm and glory "known to neither sea nor land." To those of her own age, she was sibyl and seer—a prophetess revealing the future, pointing the path, opening their eyes to the great aims only worthy of pursuit in life. To those older than herself she was . . . a wonderful union of exuberance and judgment. . . . They saw with surprise her clear good sense balancing her flow of sentiment and ardent courage. They saw her comprehension of both sides of every question and gave her their confidence, as to one of equal age, because of so ripe a judgment.

In the company of people who felt so warmly toward her, Margaret felt a measure of contentment. She was disappointed that she was, as she described herself, ugly. She was disappointed not to have the fun of flirtations and light romances. And there was always that underlying sense of differentness and melancholy. But there was good conversation, warm friends, reading, and learning. It was a pleasant time.

Timothy Fuller's disappointed ambitions, however, put an end to Margaret's contentment. When she was twenty-three, he retired from his law practice—which had never been as successful as he would have liked—and bought a farm. The life of a gentleman farmer appealed to him. He would be beholden to no man. He would cultivate his own land and feed his family from the produce of that land. He would commune with God's creation instead of having to waste his time in conversation with his inferiors. And he would have more time for his own study and writing.

But for Margaret, the move was a disaster. The farm was in Groton, and she had no desire to return to the scene of her adolescent crime at the Misses Prescott's school. Moreover, there was no railroad between Boston and Groton, and it was difficult for her to get into the city and visit with her friends. And in the town of Groton, there was no one who interested her. Instead of the stimulating companionship of bright young Boston men and women, there were only exchanges of humdrum conversation with the villagers and the hired help, and the tedious task of teaching her younger sister and brothers. All she had to keep her going was her studies and her father's promise that in time he would send her on a trip to Europe.

Even Timothy Fuller must have realized, once the excitement of the move wore off, that it was a mistake. The Fullers were townspeople, not farmers, and they were not cut out for a life of social isolation and physical labor—a life dictated by the elements, in which whole weeks might go by when they had no one to talk to but each other. Relations in the family became strained, even ugly. The two older boys began to quarrel violently with their father, and they eventually left home. Margaret was not getting along with him very well, either. Timid Mrs. Fuller could not stand the strain of constant conflict, and she escaped into frequent bouts of illness, leaving the entire management of the household to Margaret. The youngest child, a baby boy, fell ill and died.

After two years in Groton, Margaret, too, broke down. For nine days she lay in bed with a raging fever and pain so severe that she—and everyone else in the family—thought she would die. Her mother was at her bedside day and night. And her father was so overcome with concern and fear for her life that he permitted himself a luxury he had never indulged before. He spoke to Margaret not as a teacher or disciplinarian, but as a loving parent. "My dear," he said to her one morning, "I have been thinking of you in the night, and I cannot remember that you have any faults. You have defects, of course, as all mortals have, but I do not know that you have a single fault."

Finally, Margaret recovered. But her illness was not the worst calamity the Fullers had to face. Not long afterward, Timothy Fuller fell ill with cholera, and in less than a day he was dead. Margaret, at twenty-five, now became—in fact, if not in title—the head of the family: teacher and guide for her younger brothers and sister, confidante for her mother, planner for the entire family. When her father's tangled financial affairs were examined, another burden was thrust on her. He had left far less money than expected, and the family would have to live frugally and carefully in order to make ends meet.

Margaret's trip to Europe was now impossible, and she resigned herself to that fact. She resigned herself, also, to a frugal life in which even the books she loved so much had become luxuries. She resigned herself to spinsterhood and to living with her mother and her younger brothers and sister as long as they needed her.

But she could not resign herself to defeat. One day something happened that made her realize that living in Groton would eventually destroy her. She went to pay a call on some neighbors—an elderly woman and her aged mother who lived not far from the Fullers' farm. She had been to visit them before, but never had she been so struck by what greeted her—grinding, soul-destroying, hopeless poverty. She described it in her journal:

> The little room—they have but one—contains a bed, a table and some old chairs. A single stick of wood burns in the fireplace. . . . Everything is old and faded, but at the same time as clean and carefully mended as possible. . . .
>
> And there they sit—mother and daughter. In the mother, ninety years have quenched every thought and every feeling, except an imbecile interest about her daughter. Husband, sons, strength, health, house and land all are gone . . . morning by morning she rises without a hope, night by night she lies down vacant and apathetic. . . .
>
> The daughter—that bloodless effigy of humanity, whose care is to eke out this miserable existence by means of the occasional doles of those who know how faithful and good a child she has been to that decrepit creature; whose

> talk is of the price of pounds of sugar and ounces of tea, and yards of flannel; whose only intellectual resource is hearing five or six verses of the Bible read every day—"my poor head," she says, "cannot bear any more," and whose only hope is the death, to which she has been so slowly and wearily advancing, through many years like this . . . the saddest part is, that she does not wish for death. She clings to this sordid existence. . . .

Such a vision of her own future was intolerable. She could not permit it to happen. She could not stand by and watch her mother's life and her own trail off into such abject futility. She would leave Groton and go to Boston to find work as a teacher. It would mean more money for all the Fullers. And for her, it would mean a chance to live.

3

The Like-Minded

On September 22, 1834, an unusual school opened its doors in Boston. It was called the Temple School because of its location on the top floor of the Masonic Temple on Tremont Street, and its director was a gentle, idealistic, and thoroughly impractical man named Amos Bronson Alcott. Alcott came from a poor family, and had very little schooling. But he had educated himself, and his reading and experience convinced him that the conventional methods of teaching, which consisted almost exclusively of drill and discipline, were all wrong.

To Alcott, education was not a device for forcing information into children's reluctant heads, it was a way of drawing out their inherent abilities and developing their capacities for understanding, imagination, and character. There was no corporal punishment in his school; his students learned by the conversational method; they worked on an honor system; they had a kind of self-government. All of these were startling innovations.

News of the Temple Street School traveled to Margaret in Groton, and she liked what she heard. She knew how much suffering Timothy Fuller's rigidity and pressure had cost her, and she was sure she would have learned as much—and much more happily—in a free and relaxed atmosphere. So it was to Mr. Alcott that she applied when she decided to become a teacher. He met her and was impressed with her—she had, he wrote in his journal, "liberal and varied acquirements," "the rarest good sense and discretion," and an "unspoiled integrity of being"—and he promptly hired her as the Temple School's teacher of Latin and French.

Margaret moved to Boston in August of 1836 and took up her position the next month. The school was small, and the salary Alcott could afford to pay her was far too meager to enable her to support herself and at the same time send money to her mother. So she took on additional jobs. She gave private evening classes in Latin and German; she tutored a blind boy in Latin, history, and Shakespeare; one evening a week she read aloud from her own translations of the works of the German philosophers to William Ellery Channing, the well-loved pastor of the Federal Street Church. And, Margaret being Margaret, she devoted long hours to her own work, poring over plans for the book she wanted to write about the great German author Goethe, who had died just a few years before.

With such a schedule, it is not surprising that Margaret frequently felt exhausted and sick. She was overworked, she drove herself without mercy, she worried about her family in Groton. She began to be plagued by the headaches that in her adult life replaced the nightmares of her childhood. Although the headaches were usually so severe as to send her to bed, she also thought of them as a badge of honor, persuading herself that pain and suffering gave her strength and that her mind was keenest when her body was most miserable. At the same time, she had a well-developed sense of the ridiculous, and she recognized, wryly, that there was something a little foolish in her almost constant illness. "I am still quite unwell," she wrote to a friend, "and all my pursuits and propensities have a tendency to make my head worse. It is but a bad head—as bad as if I were a great man! I am not entitled to so bad a head by anything I have done, but I flatter myself that it is very interesting to suffer so much, and a fair excuse for not writing pretty letters, and saying to my friends the good things I think about them."

Margaret's headaches were not helped any by the controversy that grew up around her employer. Shortly after she arrived at the Temple School, a book of Alcott's was published that sent Boston's respectable citizens into a rage. *Conversations with Children on the Gospels* described Alcott's approach to what was called "moral education." Instead of teaching children the Bible as a series of true stories, Alcott encouraged them to develop and express their own views about the ethical and spiritual issues of the

Scriptures. For children to be permitted to have their own ideas on any subject was outrageous enough; for them to be permitted to have their own ideas about the Bible was not merely outrageous, it was blasphemous. Boston's two most powerful newspapers wrote indignant editorials against Alcott. Andrews Norton, the head of the Harvard Divinity School, attacked him publicly. Ministers inveighed against him from the pulpit.

Margaret and Elizabeth Peabody, the other Temple School teacher, rose to Alcott's defense. And two important men—Margaret's old friend James Freeman Clarke, now a minister, and Ralph Waldo Emerson, who had resigned his pastorate only a few years before—added the weight of their influence. But the defense was only partly effective, and parents, horrified by what they were hearing about Alcott, began to snatch their children from the clutches of this heretic. By April 1837, the school was near bankruptcy and Alcott had to sell all its furniture and its library. It took two years before the Temple School was finally forced to close its doors forever—this time Alcott had committed the even greater heresy of taking a black child into his school. At the end there remained as his pupils only this child and two of Alcott's daughters—Anna and Louisa, who later became one of America's most beloved writers of children's stories and books.

In April, when the Temple School crisis was reaching its climax, Margaret received a teaching offer from the Greene Street School in Providence. She had difficulty making a decision. She did not want to appear to be deserting Alcott. And she was reluctant to leave her friends and the cultural advantages of Boston; she had had quite enough of living outside the mainstream. But the offer from Providence was really too good to reject. She would be paid $1000 a year for four hours of work a day. This was an extremely generous salary for any teacher, and it was more than had ever before been offered to a woman. She would be able to send her mother a respectable sum, and she would have enough left over for herself so that she would not have to take any private students, and would have more time for her own reading, writing, and studying. In addition, the Greene Street School was a new and forward-looking institution, which seemed to be receptive to unorthodox educational ideas, and Margaret was promised free rein to teach as she chose. Finally, Alcott encouraged her to accept the offer: it was extremely doubtful whether he would have enough money to be able to pay her next year and besides, he considered it a compliment that one of his teachers had been asked. So, a year after she had arrived in Boston, Margaret departed for Providence.

Her stay there was busy. She worked hard at organizing the school and at teaching, searching out the "kernel of nobleness" she hoped to find in all her students, and gathering around her a band of admiring, starry-eyed disciples. She spent long evenings at her own work. She had dropped the idea of writing a life of Goethe; it was, she realized, impossible to do justice to this hero of hers at such a long distance from the world he had lived in. Instead, she concentrated on translating a book about him that had recently been published in Germany—Eckermann's *Conversations with Goethe*.

Even so, the time in Providence seemed like an interruption of her life, not part of it. She could feel the years dropping away behind her; she was nearly twenty-nine, and she had accomplished nothing yet. Teaching was a perfectly respectable career for a woman and her pupils' devotion was flattering, but it seemed to Margaret that her gifts entitled her to more. There was something missing—what, she did not know. So, whenever she could, she went in search of it to Boston—to visit with her friends, to talk, to go to concerts and museums. When she was in Boston she felt closer to that vague something that shimmered hazily ahead of her, waiting for her to put herself in its path.

When she had been in Providence for two school years, her family finally found a buyer for the farm at Groton. That made some money available—enough to buy a house in Jamaica Plain, right outside of Boston and enough to free Margaret from the burden of her mother's support. It was not enough to permit her to stop working, but she could move to Jamaica Plains with her family, and get on with her own life. She could be with her friends when she wanted to be, not just on special occasions.

Those friends belonged to a very special circle—one that had developed out of an evening's conversation in the fall of 1836 at the home of the Unitarian minister George Ripley and his wife, Sophia. All of them were young—in their twenties and early thirties; all of them were serious—dedicated to reading, to the art of conversation, and to the examination of ideas. They were also discontented with the state of their country. Its values seemed to them narrow, selfish, and materialistic; its religious beliefs and practices seemed to them dry and mechanical, lacking in all sense of wonder and exaltation of the spirit. Somehow, they felt, the United States was failing its original promise. Though pioneers still moved westward, taming the wilderness and building cities on the prairies, it was no longer a land of spiritual adventure and moral courage. Instead, its citizens were smug and complacent, concerned with making money and being respectable, and refusing to think for themselves.

That first meeting led to others, and soon the group became an informal club. The members came—or did not come—as the spirit moved them, and there were no officers or dues or set meeting dates. People called it the Club of the Like-Minded because, as James Freeman Clarke wrote, "no two of us thought alike." But in time, it became known as the Transcendental Club, and those associated with it became known as Transcendentalists.

At first, most Bostonians thought of the Transcendentalists merely as peculiar and pretentious, and mocked them for their high-flown intellectuality. How seriously could one take a group of people who sat down for an evening to discuss, as Alcott reported in his journal, "knowledge, memory, hope, pre-existence, faith, elements of the soul, incarnation, miracles"? If such vaporizing amused the likes of Alcott and Margaret Fuller, the Ripleys and Ralph Waldo Emerson, they were welcome to it. Serious citizens had more serious things to attend to: making money, setting an elegant table, entertaining the prosperous and the respectable—dealing with the practical things, the things that mattered in life.

For a while the Transcendentalists confined their discussions to the privacy of their own homes. But then they began to speak out in public, scolding their countrymen for their materialism, their conventionality, their uncritical acceptance of things as they were. What seemed to the good people of Boston a proper respect for the proper order of things seemed to the Transcendentalists a kind of fossilized joylessness: men and women performing all the accepted rituals of social life and of religion without recognizing for a moment the true meanings of these rituals —without coming into any direct contact with that extraordinary miracle of which they were, by their very natures, an intrinsic part—the miracle of life.

Boston had been proud of Emerson's patriotism when he called on Americans to begin to develop their own literature. "We have listened too long to the courtly muses of Europe," he said in an address he delivered to the Phi Beta Kappa Society. But a year later, he went too far. In his commencement address to the members of the graduating class of the Harvard Divinity School, Emerson attacked all the practices and principles of New England Christianity: the view of religion as a set of laws that had to be obeyed because they had been handed down by a divine authority who could be approached only through obedience. He said, in essence, that Christ's message was not his own divinity, but the divinity in every man, and that every human being could touch that spark of divinity directly, by recognizing his oneness with the world of nature:

> Jesus Christ belonged to the true race of prophets. He saw with open eye the mystery of the soul. . . . Alone in all history, he estimated the greatness of man. One man was true to what is in you and me. He saw that God incarnates himself in man, and evermore goes forth anew to take possession of his World. He said, in this jubilee of sublime emotion, "I am divine. Through me, God acts; through me, speaks. Would you see God, see me; or, see thee, when thou also thinkest as I now think." But what a distortion did his doctrine and memory suffer in the same, in the next, and the following ages! . . . The understanding caught this high chant from the poet's lips, and said, in the next age, "This was Jehovah come down out of heaven. I will kill you, if you say he was a man." The idioms of his language and the figures of his rhetoric, have usurped the place of his truth; and churches are not built on his principles, but on his tropes. . . . He spoke of miracles; for he felt that man's life was a miracle, and all that man doth, and he knew that this his daily miracle shines, as the character ascends. But the word Miracle, as pronounced by Christian churches, gives a false impression; it is Monster.

It was at this point that the wrath of the Establishment came down on the Transcendentalists. Andrews Norton, who had taught Emerson at Harvard Divinity School, accused him and his fellow Transcendentalists of attacking "principles which are the foundation of human society and human happiness," and others spoke out with equal rage.

To the Transcendentalists, the attack was only another demonstration of what was wrong in their country. Though they had grown up in a Puritan world of literal-mindedness and strict common sense, there was more than a touch of the mystic in all of them. They knew that they felt most alive when they listened to their inner voices—not to the voices of external authority. They knew that reason was only part of the human experience, and that feelings that found no easy explanation were as valid as feelings that were part of everyday life. The greatness of art and the greatness of religion, they believed, sprang from these inner voices—this intense, direct, intuitive communion with the world of nature and the divinity that it expressed. Margaret had experienced this transfiguring mystery when she was twenty-one and living in Groton, long before she met Emerson. She described it in her journal:

> It was Thanksgiving day and I was obliged to go to church or exceedingly displease my father. I almost always suffered much in church from a feeling of disunion with the hearers and dissent from the preacher, but today more than ever before, the services jarred upon me. . . .

> I walked away over the fields as fast as I could walk . . . till I came to where the trees were thick about a little pool, dark and silent. I sat down there. I did not think; all was dark and cold, and still. Suddenly, the sun shone out. . . . And, even then, passed into my thought a beam from its true sun . . . I saw there was no self; that selfishness was all folly, and the result of circumstance, that it was only because I thought self real that I suffered; that I had only to live in the idea of the ALL, and all was mine. This truth came to me, and I received it unhesitatingly; so that I was for that hour taken up into God . . . dwelling in the ineffable, the unutterable.

But although all the Transcendentalists shared this faith in truth beyond reason, and shared disapproval of things-as-they-were, they all had special fields of interest. The Ripleys, for example, were interested in social reform. Bronson Alcott's interest was in education, as was Elizabeth Peabody's. Henry David Thoreau, at twenty-one the club's youngest member, was mainly concerned with the relationship of man to nature. Ralph Waldo Emerson's abiding interest was the full and free development of the individual human spirit. Margaret's was the life of literature. So when the group met and talked together, the conversation frequently skittered in several directions at once. As William Henry Channing, one of Margaret's good friends, wrote:

> The only password of membership to this association, which had no compact, records, or officers, was a hopeful and liberal spirit; and its

chance conventions were determined solely by the desire of the caller for a "talk," or by the arrival of some guest. . . .The tone of the assemblies was cordial welcome for everyone's peculiarity, and . . . the only guest not tolerated was intolerance.

4

A Gift for Conversation

Although, like every serious-minded New Englander of her day, Margaret kept a journal, she much preferred talking to writing. "Conversation is my natural element," she once wrote. "I need to be drawn out, and never think alone, without imagining some companion." And, another time: "After all, this writing is mighty dead. Oh, for my dear old Greeks, who talked everything—not to shine as in the Parisian saloons, but to learn, to teach, to vent the heart, to clear the mind."

But when she talked, she *did* shine, and the pleasure it gave her to converse was no greater than the pleasure her conversation gave her listeners. Bronson Alcott called her "the most brilliant talker of the day." James Freeman Clarke was even more enthusiastic. "All her friends will unite," he wrote, "in the testimony, that whatever they may have known of wit and eloquence in others, they have never seen one who, like her, by the conversation of an hour or two, could not merely entertain and inform, but make an epoch in one's life." And others who knew her agreed with these assessments.

Margaret could not help but be aware of her gifts as a conversationalist. She knew how to phrase her thoughts and feelings precisely, lucidly, and with wit and distinction. She knew how to listen to—and really hear—what others were saying and to draw them out and help them refine their own feelings and thoughts. These abilities were among the qualities that had made her such a successful teacher and had won her so many friends. So when she left Providence, she began to cast around for ways of putting her conversational gifts to work.

While she was in Providence, the popular novelist John Neal had spoken to Margaret's students about the role of women in America, and although she had some quarrels with the way he presented his argument, she was impressed with the points he made. His talk set her thinking more seriously than she had before about the problems of her sex. She had many close women friends, with whom she had a strong sense of kinship, but she had always thought of herself as different from them in many ways—set apart and stigmatized by her early training and her character, and doomed to lead a difficult and unfulfilled life.

On the other hand, she realized that some of the hardships she suffered were due entirely to her sex. If she had been a man, the world would have offered her many more outlets for her talents; it would have admired the "braininess" it did not like in her; it would have overlooked her deficiencies in beauty; it would have admired her assertiveness and even her idiosyncrasies. "A man's ambition with a woman's heart," she once wrote, "is an evil lot." And now it struck her forcefully that this evil lot was not hers alone—that her problems were those of all women. Women were held back by their society, kept as rigidly in their places as children were in theirs. Once women had finished their formal schooling, they were expected to give up all thought of anything save domesticity. Their minds and their interests were supposed simply to stop growing; they were supposed to wrap themselves in the cocoons of their homes and find all their contentment there. And even if some women managed—or were compelled—by their own characters or by the force of circumstances to escape these constraints and to participate actively in their society, that did not change the essential facts. Women were a deprived sex. They had a right to fuller, less restricted lives. They had a right to expand their interests beyond their homes.

A somewhat similar thought had occurred to Margaret's friend Elizabeth Peabody, during the years that Margaret was trapped in Groton. Elizabeth was distressed by the lack of educational opportunities for women, and she had organized a series of Reading Parties—evening gatherings at which interested Boston women came together at various private homes to discuss, under her leadership, important books and ideas. But Elizabeth's interest had been in women's education. Margaret's was in women's lives—in giving women the intellectual tools that would enable them to put their education and their gifts to use.

When Margaret combined the thoughts that John Neal's lecture had sparked in her with the Reading Parties that Elizabeth had held, a plan for earning her living took form in her mind. She described it in a letter to Sophia Ripley:

> Could a circle [of women] be assembled in earnest, desirous to answer the questions—what were we born to do? and how shall we do it?—which so few ever propose to themselves till their best years are gone by, I should think the undertaking a noble one and if my resources should prove sufficient to make me its moving spring, I should be willing to give it a large portion of these coming years which will, I hope, be my best. . . .

There was no question, Margaret pointed out, that such a project was needed

> to supply a point of union to well-educated and thinking women, in a city which, with great pretensions to mental refinement, boasts, at present, nothing of the kind . . . to systematize thought and give a precision and clearness in which our sex are so deficient, chiefly, I think, because they have so few inducements to test and classify what they receive; to ascertain

> what pursuits are best suited to us, in our time and state of society, and how we may make best use of our means for building up the life of thought upon the life of action. . . .

Sophia and the other women to whom Margaret broached the idea were enthusiastic, and the project was soon under way. At noon on November 6, 1839, twenty-five women gathered at Elizabeth Peabody's rooms on West Street, and the first of Margaret's Conversations began. The group was distinguished; it included some of the brightest and most talented women in Massachusetts. Among them were the three Peabody sisters—Elizabeth, Mary, and Sophia; Margaret's old friend and mentor Eliza Farrar; her young friend Caroline Sturgis; Lidian Emerson, Ralph Waldo Emerson's wife, who had driven in from the Emersons' home in Concord; Sarah Clarke, James Freeman Clarke's sister; Sophia Ripley; and young Maria White, who was engaged to the poet James Russell Lowell. All of them had been drawn together by their desire to sharpen their minds and their understanding, and by their admiration for the woman who was to lead them.

Margaret had prepared herself carefully, studying and planning for this discussion and searching for ways to set the tone for all the discussions that would follow. The dissatisfaction with her appearance that had led her, when she was at the Misses Prescott's school, to rouge her cheeks, had blossomed as she matured into a meticulous concern for her dress, and whenever she appeared in public she was always elegantly, even sumptuously costumed, usually in dresses made at home, since she could seldom afford the expense of a dressmaker. Now she swept dramatically into the room, escorted by Elizabeth. The whispers and the rustlings stopped. Everyone was still.

This first series of Conversations, to run for thirteen weeks, was on the subject of Greek mythology, but before Margaret launched into the subject proper, she explained her larger purposes—purposes that far transcended any of the specific topics the women might discuss.

> Women are now taught at school all that men are. They run over superficially even *more* studies, without being really taught anything. But with this difference: men are called on from a very early period to reproduce all that they learn. Their college exercises, their political duties, their professional studies, the first actions of life in any direction, call on them to put to use what they have learned. But women learn without any attempt to reproduce. Their only reproduction is for purposes of display. It is to supply this defect that these conversations have been planned.

The Conversations were an instant success. For most of the women, it was a new and exciting experience to have their ideas taken seriously, and to be encouraged to think and express themselves—and Margaret did encourage them. As one of the participants wrote: "Whatever was said, Margaret knew how to seize the good meaning of it with hospitality, and to make the speaker feel glad, and not sorry, that she had spoken." In such an encouraging atmosphere, the women could literally feel their minds growing. And they could feel, too, a new sense of community with one another and a new sense of the worth of their sex.

By the second season, their success had made the Conversations themselves a topic of conversation in Boston, and Margaret had become something of a celebrity, praised for her brilliance, her erudition, and her force of character. But not everything that was said about her or the Conversations was flattering. Her assistants—as she called the women in the group—were criticized for being affected, for not "knowing their places," for being dabblers, for wasting their time—and their husbands' money. And Margaret was criticized simply for being Margaret. Her dramatic manner and her intensity made her a perfect target: it was easy to poke fun at her elegant clothes, her long neck, her nearsighted blinking, her elevated aspirations—even her spinsterhood.

But she and her assistants continued undaunted. The Conversations filled a real need for them, and they were not going to be put off. The series on mythology was followed by one on the fine arts, another on ethics, another on education, and still another on woman—her place in the family, the school, the church, and society. Every fall, and again in the spring, for the four years she remained in Boston, Margaret and her assistants—whose numbers grew as word of the Conversations got around—

would gather to begin their thirteen weeks' adventure into a world beyond their homes.

Only once was the smooth flow of the project interrupted. During the second season, some of the men in Margaret's circle, impressed by what they had heard about the Conversations, began to ask for permission to attend, and in March 1841 Margaret opened a special evening series for both men and women. Ralph Waldo Emerson, Bronson Alcott, James Freeman Clarke, and George Ripley all paid their twenty dollars for the ten sessions. But the series was not successful, and its first season was also its last. Part of the reason was that the men were far more sure of themselves intellectually than the women and tended to monopolize the discussion and to divert it from its original course into areas in which they were particularly interested and expert. In the face of this, the women became increasingly intimidated, self-conscious, and embarrassed, and retreated into what one of them called "dullness."

Nor did things improve much when they managed, with Margaret's encouragement, to overcome their fears and assert themselves. Then, the men's reactions were, in Margaret's eyes, patronizing and arrogant. It seemed to her that there was insult even in their praise. "Their encomiums," she wrote, "are always in some sense mortifying: they show too much surprise. 'Can this be you?' he cries to the transfigured Cinderella; 'well, I should never have thought it, but I am very glad. . . . We will tell everyone that you have surpassed your sex.' "

Such an accusation would have startled and even

offended the men in the group. They were, indeed, among the most liberal and open-minded men of their time, and it simply would never have occurred to them that, at the very least, they were being inconsiderate, and that their lack of consideration concealed a lack of respect for women's abilities. But in fact their whole society was constructed around the notion that the world was man's domain, not woman's, and unwittingly all of them accepted that assumption. Sophia Ripley, Elizabeth Peabody, and Margaret might meet with them as equals in gatherings of the Transcendentalists—but these were extraordinary women with special advantages. Sophia Ripley's place was made by her marriage: it was at her home that the first Transcendentalist meeting had taken place. Elizabeth Peabody's was made in part by her close professional association with Bronson Alcott and in part by her means of livelihood: she had converted the front room of her house on West Street into a shop where all kinds of books and magazines, unavailable anywhere else in Boston, were sold. Margaret had her brilliance and her erudition. And she also had intensity and self-assertiveness, two qualities which made it almost impossible to ignore her and which were guaranteed to set New England teeth on edge.

Certainly she upset and even put off Ralph Waldo Emerson when he first met her at Eliza Farrar's home in Cambridge in 1835. Emerson had heard of her as a prodigy, but although her wit impressed him, he did not quite approve of her. "I fancied her too much interested in personal history," he wrote of that meeting, "and her talk was a comedy in which dramatic justice was done to everybody's foibles. . . . She made me laugh more than I liked." But, as he himself said of her, "persons were her game," and he was a lion she had made up her mind to capture. If wit and pointed comments about New England's stuffier citizens did not do the trick, she would try another tack. She was, as Emerson wrote, "too intent on establishing a good footing between us to omit any art of winning. She studied my tastes, piqued and amused me, challenged frankness by frankness and did not conceal the good opinion of me she brought with her, nor her wish to please. . . . It was impossible long to hold out against such urgent assault."

The friendship between Margaret and Waldo, as she called him, began to take shape during a two-week visit Margaret made to the Emersons' home in Concord in the summer of 1836, just before she went off to Providence. That momentous first meeting of the Like-Minded had not yet taken place, but Emerson had already finished work on his first book, *Nature*, which became the closest thing the Transcendentalists had to a bible. One passage in it must certainly have spoken with particular eloquence to Margaret: the luminous, almost ecstatic experience it described virtually paralleled her own experience of five years earlier, when she was returning from church that gloomy Thanksgiving Day. "Standing on the bare ground," Emerson had written, "my head bathed by the blithe air, and uplifted into infinite space—all mean egotism vanishes. I become a transparent eyeball. I am nothing; I see all; the currents of the Universal Being circulate through me; I am part or parcel of God."

Two people who shared such an experience and such a sense of exaltation could not but be attracted to each other. But the temperamental differences between them were considerable. Emerson was a philosopher—contemplative, quiet, restrained, and moderate. Margaret was dramatic, intense—almost flamboyant.

Emerson had recovered from the tragedy of his first marriage—the wife whom he loved so deeply had died at twenty, only a year and a half after the wedding—and he had found a second wife, Lidian, who was as devoted to him as he was to her. He had given up his first career, as a minister, and was already successfully embarked on his second, as a man of letters. He was a man who had found himself.

Margaret was still in search of herself. She longed to find a man who could be more than a friend to her; she longed to become a mother—and she felt sure that these elemental needs of her womanhood would never be satisfied. She longed, too, to make a name for herself and find a career that could bring her satisfaction. Emerson had a strong sense of mysticism and of mystery, but he had an equally strong scorn for what he considered superstition. And Margaret was a bundle of quirky, odd beliefs—that the month of September was unlucky for her; that coincidences had a deeper meaning; that when she turned her head to one side, she had second sight; that at times a demonic spirit ruled her; that certain gems had powers—it delighted her that her name signified a pearl: an exquisite, delicate object wrought from the depths and from disease.

Emerson lived his life day by day, in a satisfying, steady, regular routine. Margaret woke up happy and in high spirits, and by midafternoon was usually in agony, with a headache so blinding that it sent her to her bed. "Her life," Emerson wrote about her, "concentrated itself in certain happy days, happy hours, happy moments. The rest was a void."

Such differences inevitably made for tension between them. Much as he liked and admired her, Emerson always found Margaret just a little more than he could easily take. And she, who knew this, seemed to find a perverse pleasure in shaking him up. She kept trying to coax from him more temperament and passion than he had. Their friendship was an almost constant duel, each trying to catch the other off guard; each defending against the other's thrusts—and sometimes going to extraordinary lengths in the effort. Once, when Margaret went to spend some time with Waldo and Lidian in Concord, she remained in her room for the entire visit—emerging only to take her meals—and she and Waldo kept in touch with each other through letters hand-delivered from room to room by his young son.

But in spite of all this, their friendship grew and developed, until by the time Margaret moved to Jamaica Plains and began the Conversations, they had come to accept their incompatibilities, and were willing to take the risk of becoming colleagues as well as friends.

5

A Voice for Transcendentalists

In the summer of 1840, the Transcendentalists launched their major project—a new magazine called the *Dial*. The *Dial* filled a real need for them. The two most influential journals of the day—the *North American Review* and the *Christian Examiner*—were outraged by the Transcendentalists and their ideas. The Newness was apparently much too new for these voices of the intellectual and religious Establishment, and they refused to accept any of the manuscripts the Transcendentalists submitted. The *Christian Examiner* even lashed out in an editorial against "this new form of philosophy, which is turning the heads of our American scholars, inflating some and dementing others," and which would, if unchecked, "dethrone prudence and reason and worship an indefinable spontaneity."

Such a cautious, self-protective, narrow view appalled Margaret and her Transcendentalist friends. So it is not surprising that they should have wanted to publish a journal of their own—a journal that would stand for the liberal, questioning, idealistic spirit in which they felt their country to be so deficient.

They began talking about it almost from the moment of their first meeting at the Ripleys' home. But planning, organization, and management were never among the Transcendentalists' strong points, and it took them nearly three years to get the project off the ground. Emerson had been its guiding light from the start, but when the vague plans showed promise of becoming a reality, Margaret was named editor. Emerson continued his interest in the project, but he preferred, at least in the beginning, to work behind the scenes. Besides, Margaret needed the two hundred dollars yearly the job was supposed to pay, and she had talents to bring to the enterprise that few of the others possessed. There was her talent for friendship. It had grown as she grew, until now, as Emerson put it, "she wore [her] circle of friends as a necklace of diamonds about her neck." She had a gift for entering into other people's interests and enthusiasms, and she could, therefore, choose contributions that would make the *Dial* reflect the breadth and diversity of views among the Like-Minded. Then there was her literary background. A number of literary articles and poems were to be included in each of the four issues of the magazine published yearly, and Margaret had a wider knowledge of literature than any of the other Transcendentalists. Literature was, in fact, her deepest and oldest interest, and, from the time she was a child, she had been writing out her critical response to everything she read.

Finally, with all her contempt for materialism, Margaret had a very strong sense of the practical. After all, she had been supporting herself and guiding her family ever since her father's death. If any of the Transcendentalists could be counted on to turn a dream into a publication, it was Margaret.

She set to work on the *Dial* with all her energies. She bombarded her friends with letters requesting contributions; since not enough of them came in which were of an acceptable quality, she wrote and wrote herself: eight of the pieces in the first issue were hers, some of them unsigned. She engaged in long discussions—even arguments—with Emerson about the editorial that was to introduce the magazine to its readers. They agreed, on the whole, about what it was to say, but they disagreed about how to say it. Their writing styles reflected their temperaments: Margaret's was dramatic and extravagant; Waldo's was calm and understated. She would have liked to strike out at her countrymen for their Philistinism; he preferred a more moderate tone. And he won the argument; the *Dial*'s introductory editorial was largely written by Emerson. It was sharp enough in its criticism, bemoaning that "rigor of our conventions and education which is turning us to stone, which renounces hope, which looks only backward, which asks only such a future as the past, which suspects improvement, and holds nothing so much in horror as new views or the dreams of youth." And it described the rebels against that rigor as united in "a common love of truth, and love of its work," who had a "greater trust in the nature and resources of man than the laws or the popular opinion will well allow."

By the time those words appeared in print, Margaret was in a state of total exhaustion. It had been a difficult year for her. There was the demanding job of getting the magazine together—of soliciting material, reading it, evaluating it, editing it, and writing her own pieces. There were the struggles with Emerson over the introductory editorial. And there were the Conversations. Each session may have lasted only two hours, but Margaret spent considerably more time than that in preparation. And there were her headaches—those blinding agonies that had by now become her almost constant companions.

In addition to all this, there was a wrenching personal crisis—one that put all Margaret's expectations of herself to the test. About two years earlier, she had—to her surprise and joy—finally fallen in love. His name was Samuel Gray Ward, and he was witty, charming, and seven years younger than she. Sam had studied in Germany and traveled throughout Europe, and had become familiar, at firsthand, with all the exciting literary, artistic, and intellectual movements that were springing into life there. He shared Margaret's passion for Goethe, whose works and character the conventional wisdom denounced as immoral. He had seen some of the world's great paintings in Paris and in Rome, and had returned home with a huge portfolio of engravings of some of the masterpieces of European art and architecture —masterpieces Margaret saw for the first time when she met him.

It was inevitable that Sam and Margaret should be attracted to each other, and that Margaret should finally dare to hope she had found the man who could keep the key to her character. She did not confide in anyone, but her more perceptive friends suspected that her emotions were deeply involved in Sam. Sam was, Emerson wrote, Margaret's "companion and . . . guide in the study of art . . . and [they] long kept up a profuse correspondence on books and studies in which they had a mutual interest. And yet," he continued, "these literary sympathies, though sincere, were only veils and occasions to beguile the time, so profound was her interest in the character and fortunes of her friend."

But the romance was a doomed one. Sam's wit and brilliance matched Margaret's, but his dedication to an intellectual life did not. He came from a family of bankers—people who, in Margaret's words, were "more anxious to get a living than to live mentally and morally," and they expected him to enter the family business. He put up a feeble protest: he had planned to devote his life to literature. But in the end he gave in and joined the family firm.

Margaret was sickened. This was worse than weakness, it was treachery. "All I loved in you," she wrote him, "is at present dead and buried; only a light from the tomb shines now and then in your eyes." But it was easier to write the words than to erase the feelings. She could not forget his wit, his charm, her hopes. She felt devastated—and more alone and isolated than ever before.

Then her misery was compounded. A few years before, Eliza Farrar had introduced Sam to a cousin of her husband's—a young New Yorker named Anna Barker. Anna was beautiful and charming; she was about Sam's age, and, like him, she came from a wealthy family. Margaret already knew Anna—indeed, she had known her for over ten years. When Margaret was eighteen, and still living in Cambridge, Anna's parents had sent their daughter to spend some time with the Farrars, in the hope that they could add luster to Anna's beauty by introducing her to the cultivated world of New England intellectualism. Margaret seemed to Eliza a perfect mentor for Anna, and she brought the two young women together. They took to each other instantly and became inseparable. Anna looked up to Margaret with awed admiration, and Margaret felt more affection for this delightful woman than for any of her other protégées. Even after Anna left Cambridge, their warm friendship continued.

For a while after their first meeting, Anna and Sam were friends, and nothing more—two people drawn together at least in part by their shared admiration and affection for Margaret. But they came from the same world, and her beauty complemented his wit. In time, they fell in love.

Margaret heard the news of their engagement in the summer of 1840, just as the first issue of the *Dial* was ready to go on press. She took it hard. It had been nearly a year since she had written Sam the letter that cancelled him out of her life. It had been more than ten years since the period of her real intimacy with Anna. But the old feelings about both of them were still there. And there was still the feeling of her own unworthiness—her "ugliness," which contrasted with Anna's beauty; her assertiveness, which contrasted with Anna's gentler nature, and which made her, or so she thought, unlovable. And inevitably there must have been anger, and the same sense of rejection and desire for revenge that had overwhelmed her at the Misses Prescott's school.

This welter of conflicting emotions would have been terrifying to anyone. But to Margaret, it was almost unbearable. Worst of all was the rage, which was to her only another demonstration of the infinite distance between her character and the perfection she demanded of herself. She isolated herself from all her friends. "I remain fixed to be as much alone as possible," she wrote in her journal. "It is best for me. I am not fitted to be loved. . . ."

Emerson worried about her. She had, he wrote, "passed into certain religious states which did not impress me as quite healthy." Waldo knew, out of his own experience, the blissful feeling of direct communion with God. But he had no experience of the darker side of life; he had no demons that needed exorcism. Margaret did—and those religious states her friend distrusted were her effort to expunge the blackness from her soul. By the time the summer was over, she had succeeded so well that she was able to conceal any traces of the blackness from one of her oldest friends.

The friend was William Henry Channing. Channing was one of the young Harvard students who had been part of Margaret's circle when they were all in their teens, but he had left Boston shortly after he finished his education, and he did not return until the summer of 1840. One of the first things he did on his arrival was to go out to Jamaica Plain to see Margaret. He knew nothing of her aborted romance, and nothing in her behavior gave him any clue to it. On the contrary, he found Margaret as brilliant and witty as ever. She described to him the history and meaning of every one of the engravings in the drawing room of her new home; she took him on a walk through the garden and discoursed to him on the shrubs and flowers she had always loved so much. Channing enjoyed every moment of it. Margaret's conversation had always had the power to enchant her listeners.

But something in her manner told him that all these words were merely introduction—that she had not yet said what she really wanted to say:

> Nearer and nearer, Margaret was approaching a secret throned in her heart . . . and the preceding transitions were but a prelude of her orchestra before the entrance of the festal group. Unconsciously, she made these preparations for paying worthy honors to a high sentiment. She had lately heard of the betrothal of two of her best-loved friends, and she wished

> to communicate the graceful story in a way that should do justice to the facts and to her own feelings. . . .

Margaret had not merely exorcised a demon. She had performed an act of alchemy. She had transmuted her pain and anger into joy for the joy of her friends.

6

Brook Farm

While Margaret was wrestling with the demons of her character, her friend George Ripley was engaged in a different kind of struggle. He was, at the time, pastor of the Purchase Street Unitarian Church in Boston, and had been since 1826, the year he graduated from the Harvard Divinity School. Unitarianism had begun only a few years before he entered the ministry, as a protest against the rigid and self-righteous Calvinism of the Congregational Church; it rejected the Calvinist belief in an elect and in predestination in favor of the more optimistic belief that man could save himself by his works.

But as time passed, Ripley became increasingly dissatisfied with the church and its role. The liberal and hopeful spirit with which Unitarianism had begun seemed to him to be fading fast. He believed that the purpose of Christianity was not only to redeem the individual, but to redeem society, and he saw no evidence at all that the church was performing this mission. One of his hopes for the meeting at his home in the fall of 1836 had been that the group gathered there would help press the church to fulfill its social responsibility.

Everyone at that meeting—and all the others who later joined the Transcendentalist group—were as discontented with orthodox Unitarianism and the state of American society as Ripley was, but few of them shared his commitment to social action. Margaret had little confidence in efforts to change society; she believed, as she had written, in "trying to quicken the soul . . . [to] work from within outward." Emerson found the whole idea of social action uncongenial. And others had their own concerns.

Still Ripley persisted. A severe depression was sweeping the country, and all around him he saw people without work or even food—there were women begging in the streets of Boston. He was appalled by the extremes of wealth and poverty in his country, by the artificial distinction between mental and physical labor, and by the notions of master and servant. All these seemed to him to contradict both the spirit of the Republic and the spirit of Christianity. If all men were created equal, all men should share equally in the good things of life; if the meek were blessed and the earth theirs to inherit, then they should be able to claim at least one plot of land.

In the summer of 1840, after he had performed his last chore of readying the first issue of the *Dial* for publication—for he worked with Margaret and Waldo, as the managing editor—Ripley and his wife, Sophia, rented a farm in West Roxbury, nine miles from Boston. It was a beautiful place: "birds and trees, sloping green hills and hay fields as far as the eye can see," Sophia wrote to a friend, "and a brook clear running, at the foot of a green bank . . . sings us to our rest with its quiet tune, and chants its morning song to the rising sun." In this peaceful spot, the Ripleys assessed their past and planned their future. They were not far from Jamaica Plain and occasionally, when Margaret was willing to emerge from her solitude, they would visit of an evening to discuss their hopes with her.

For George had finally come to a decision. After nearly fifteen years of service, he was going to resign his pulpit and devote himself to the Christian mission to redeem society—at least in some small part. The farm he and Sophia were renting was up for sale, and he wanted to buy it and turn it into a self-supporting cooperative community, where families—and single people—could live and work and raise their children, all as equals, sharing the labor and the rewards equally. He outlined the plan in a letter to Emerson.

> Our objects, as you know, are to ensure a more natural union between intellectual and manual labor than now exists; to combine the thinker and the worker, as far as possible, in the same individual; to guarantee the highest mental freedom, by providing all with labor, adapted to

> their tastes and talents, and securing to them the fruits of their industry; to do away with the necessity of menial services, by opening the benefits of education and the profits of labor to all; and thus to prepare a society of liberal, intelligent and cultivated persons, whose relations with each other would permit a more simple and wholesome life, than can be led amidst the pressure of our competitive institutions.
>
> To accomplish these objects, we propose to take a small tract of land, which, under skillful husbandry, uniting the garden and the farm, will be adequate to the subsistence of the families; and to connect with this a school or college, in which the most complete instruction shall be given, from the first rudiments to the highest culture. Our farm would be a place for improving the race of men that lived on it; thought would preside over the operations of labor, and labor would contribute to the expansion of thought; we should have industry without drudgery, and true equality without its vulgarity.

Emerson sympathized with Ripley's ideals, but he was unwilling to join the community: the last thing in the world he wanted was to exchange the privacy and independence of his life with Lidian for a fishbowl existence of enforced sociability. And there was his distaste for the way the project was to be organized. Ripley proposed to finance the purchase of the farm and the necessary equipment by forming a joint-stock company, with shares selling at five hundred dollars apiece and the farm's profits, if any, to be apportioned among the stockholders. Although his letter spoke of carrying the "divine idea" into effect and bringing "a light over this country and this age," Waldo believed that the proposal smacked far less of God than of Mammon. "I wished to be convinced," he wrote in his journal, "to be thawed, to be made nobly mad by the kindlings before my eyes of a new dawn of human piety. But the scheme was arithmetic and comfort . . . a room in the Astor House hired for the Transcendentalists."

If Emerson thought the project too worldly, Margaret's concern was that it was not worldly enough. She knew what her father's experiment in farming had cost all the Fullers, and she had very little confidence that city intellectuals could transform themselves into sturdy peasants. "He is too sanguine," she wrote to a friend about Ripley, "and does not take time to let things ripen in his mind. . . ." But despite her doubts about Ripley's practicality, and despite her personal unwillingness to return to the rural life she had despised in Groton, she was still a romantic and found something enormously appealing in the dream of the perfect society and the simple life. Only a few days earlier, while visiting with a friend in the country, she had fantasized her own utopia, and written about it in her journal:

> A few friends should settle upon the banks of a stream . . . planting their homesteads. Some should be farmers, some woodmen, others bakers, millers, and etc. By land they should carry

> to one another the commodities; on the river they should meet for society. At sunset many, of course, would be out in their boats, but they would love the hour too much ever to disturb one another. . . . I would invite select friends to live thru the noon of night, in silent communion. When we wanted to have merely playful chat, or talk on politics or social reform, we would gather in the mill, and arrange those affairs while grinding the corn. What a happy place for children to grow up in! . . .
>
> One thing seems sure—that many persons will soon, somehow, somewhere, throw off a part at least of these terrible weights of the social contract and see if they cannot live more at ease in the lap of nature. . . .

Indeed, many people were already throwing off those weights. Many communes of one sort or another were already in existence. Since long before the Revolution, immigrants had been arriving in search of religious freedom, whose beliefs called on them to establish communities of their own. Just about the time George Ripley was finishing Harvard Divinity School, a wealthy English social reformer named Robert Owen had established New Harmony, a large cooperative in Indiana with more than a thousand members. It lasted only two years: the dreamers and intellectuals it attracted could not make a go of it on the land. The religious communities lasted far longer. But all of them demanded strict adherence to a specific belief and a specific way of living. The philosophy of Brook Farm, as Ripley's community came to be known, was far less restrictive. The Like-Minded had never demanded like-mindedness, and for the first years of its existence, Brook Farm was a joyous Babel that came close to fulfilling Margaret's dream.

It started inauspiciously in April of 1841. There were not even twenty people, including children, and only three—Frank Farley, William Allen, and Elise Barker—had any real experience of life on a farm. The rest were townspeople—and not merely townspeople, but intellectuals, brought up in a genteel, middle-class tradition, and unused to any kind of physical labor. One of them was Elizabeth Peabody's future brother-in-law, an unsuccessful writer named Nathaniel Hawthorne, who had left his job at the Boston Custom House and joined the community in the hope that it would provide a place for him and his bride-to-be, Sophia, to live when they were married—a place where he could farm by day, to earn their living, and write in the evenings. He had even dipped into his very meager savings and purchased two shares in the company, as a token of his commitment to this new way of life. But he had no illusions about his competence as a farmer, and poked fun at his ignorance and clumsiness in a letter to Sophia only days after his arrival:

> I did not milk the cows last night because Mr. Ripley was afraid to trust them to my hands, or me to their horns—I know not which. But this morning, I have done wonders. Before breakfast, I went out to the barn, and began to

> chop hay for the cattle; and with such righteous vehemence (as Mr. Ripley says) did I labor that, in the space of ten minutes, I broke the machine. Then I brought wood and replenished the fires; and finally sat down to breakfast and ate up a huge mound of buckwheat cakes. After breakfast, Mr. Ripley put a four-pronged instrument into my hands, which he gave me to understand was called a pitchfork; and he and Mr. Farley being armed with similar weapons, we all commenced a gallant attack upon a heap of manure. The affair being concluded, and thy husband having purified himself, he sits down to finish this letter to his most beloved wife.

But the Brook Farmers' inexperience was compensated by their enthusiasm, and by the time Elizabeth came to visit two weeks later, the fields had been plowed and planted, the milk yield had been increased by a third, and everyone was full of excited confidence. Already, new members were expected—among them Margaret's friend William Henry Channing and her youngest brother, Lloyd, who was to work on the farm and study at the school, so that he would be prepared to enter Harvard in the fall.

And from that point, Brook Farm grew apace, with more members joining daily—at one point there were more than a hundred. The men worked in the fields, or at trades; the women cooked, baked, sewed, scrubbed—and taught: the three schools—nursery, primary, and college preparatory—were under Sophia Ripley's direction. Women taught most of the courses and were entirely in charge of the youngest children. The crops flourished, and there was even a surplus to sell at market in Boston. Brook Farm attracted the brightest and most adventurous young people in New England—a second generation of those first eager Transcendentalists. No work was too hard for them, no idea was too unorthodox for examination, and the atmosphere seemed all joy. The men grew beards and wore blue cotton tunics, cowhide boots over their trousers, and visored caps; the women wore knickerbockers and short skirts and decorated their wide-brimmed hats with flowers, berries, and vine leaves. By night, they relaxed at lectures on philosophy, astronomy, botany, and vegetarianism; at readings of Shakespeare; at amateur theatricals; at dances and pageants. There were drives to Boston to listen to concerts; there were weekend picnics and boating on the river.

Visitors came frequently—and Margaret was one of the most honored. In this community of equals, there was always some young woman who idolized Miss Fuller, and desired nothing more than to be allowed to wait on her. She would happily give up her room to this celebrated visitor, cleaning it thoroughly before Margaret's arrival and bringing Miss Fuller her morning coffee in bed, in Brook Farm's only elegant china cup, while everyone else was at breakfast in the communal dining hall.

Margaret repaid this special treatment by offering Conversations. But the atmosphere at the farm was far different from the atmosphere at Elizabeth Peabody's West Street shop. Although, as Margaret wrote after one weekend at Brook Farm, her audience "showed on the whole more respect and interest than I had expected," they demonstrated little of the decorum of city matrons. "The people showed a great deal of the *sans-culotte* tendency in their manners, throwing themselves on the floor, yawning, and going out when they had had enough." In the face of such a reception, it is not surprising that she rejected Sophia Ripley's repeated invitations to stay at the farm for longer periods and to serve as the community's resident "genius." She would feel, she explained, in the "same position the clergyman is in, or the wandering beggar with his harp. Each day you must prove yourself anew . . ." The strain of proving herself to herself each day was enough for Margaret; she was not going to undertake the additional strain of proving herself to a group of communards. It was enough for her to visit the farm occasionally, to enjoy its physical beauty—and to give Conversations when the time seemed right and the people genuinely interested.

Brook Farm quickly lost its romance for Hawthorne. Farm work soon became drudgery—drudgery that so tired him he had no energy left to write. Sparkling conversations with bright young communards soon seemed to him to lose their effervescence. Margaret, especially, annoyed him, and in one of his letters to Sophia he described one of Brook Farm's cows as "the transcendental heifer belonging to Miss Margaret Fuller. She is very fractious, I believe, and apt to kick over the pail. Thou knowest best whether in these traits of character she resembles her mistress." Six months of communal living was all that Hawthorne could take. But he was among the very few malcontents in those early days when Brook Farm seemed indeed to be a dream come true.

Later, however, discontent became more widespread, and the Farm lost its exuberant youth. Ripley had always been interested in the ideas of the French social philosopher Charles Fourier, and in 1844 he decided to put them into effect at Brook Farm. Fourier's vision of the ideal society was based on two notions: that of "attractive industry"—by which he meant that each person should be allowed to do the kind of work he most enjoyed; and that of the phalanx—the smallest number of people that could be organized to get all the necessary work done. To assure that his scheme would work, Fourier had devised a series of complex organizational rules.

Fourier's dedication to equality was extremely attractive to American idealists and social reformers. The growth of cities and of industry meant that thousands of people were living unrewarding, impoverished lives—crowded into small, dark slum houses and toiling all day in factories at boring and backbreaking work—while a small handful of their countrymen were living in luxury. That was a far cry from the equalitarian dreams that had guided the founders of the country. So Fourier's plan to return the people to the land, return dignity to manual labor, and do away with artificial class distinctions found many followers.

But the organization of Brook Farm into a phalanx —with its subdivisions into series and groups—

proved to be unworkable. First of all, the community was too small. And then, there were so many rules that had to be followed, so many organizational complexities that had to be dealt with. The spontaneity that had been the farm's greatest asset began to disappear. Instead of conversations on all kinds of subjects, the Brook Farmers were now treated to long lectures on Fourierist doctrine. Instead of Transcendentalist talk about "affinities," there was Fourierist analysis of the "law of groups and series." Instead of cheerful disagreement, there was sullen unanimity.

And then, in March of 1846, the catastrophe occurred that spelled the end of the Ripleys' utopia. The farmers had been working for months erecting a new building—the Phalanstery—which was to provide a center for Brook Farm. It went up in flames and was completely destroyed. That took the heart out of the remaining Brook Farmers, and early in the next year the project was abandoned.

7
Summer on the Lakes

By the spring of 1843, Margaret was bone-tired. She had been back in Boston for four years now, and working constantly—driven by her own demanding character and by the necessity of earning a living. There were the Conversations every week, which required long hours of preparation. There was her own work: in a little more than two years she translated two books from the German and saw them through to publication. And there was the *Dial*. She had given up the editorship, but she was still close to it, continuing to write articles and to consult with Emerson, who had taken over the job, whenever he asked her to.

To add to all this, there was the emotional burden of her family. It was becoming lighter, but it was still there. Her favorite brother, Eugene, had left home and struck out on his own before their father died, and her brothers Arthur and Richard were finally close to independence—one finishing law school, the other training for the ministry. Her young sister, Ellen, had just gotten married to another nephew of old William Ellery Channing, who bore the same name as his uncle. Ellery was charming, a poet, and irresponsible. Although Margaret was delighted for her sister's happiness, she was far from sure it would last. Another concern was her youngest brother, Lloyd, who had been sent to Brook Farm to prepare him for Harvard. Lloyd was something of a problem. He was a poor student, and poor at getting along with other people: in fact, a confused and troublesome young man who finally had to be sent to an institution for the mentally disturbed. And there was her mother—sweet and gentle, but ineffectual—entirely dependent on Margaret's judgment and guidance.

Margaret felt crushed under the same sense of oppression that had weighed her down when, in Groton, she had visited the old woman and her daughter. It seemed to her that she was caught in a changeless eternity: her life would always be devoted to doing what she had to do, not what she wanted to, and not what she could do, if her powers were set free.

So she was pleased by the invitation James Freeman Clarke extended to her. He and his sister Sarah, a talented painter who was among the most devoted of Margaret's assistants at the Conversations, were taking a summer trip westward, across the Great

Lakes, as far as the Wisconsin territory. Would Margaret like to go with them? And with the invitation, James enclosed fifty dollars. He knew that Margaret would not be able to afford the trip otherwise. Nor did he mention the money—which made it easier for Margaret to accept. The prospect of getting away for a while and seeing some more of the country delighted her. Her longest expedition outside New England had been in the summer of 1835, when Eliza Farrar rescued her from Groton for a short time, taking her on a journey down the Atlantic coast to Newport, New York, and New Jersey. But the West was the land of promise to Americans. Daily, people were deserting New England to build new lives on the frontier.

The travelers left Boston early in June, and by the tenth of the month had arrived at Niagara Falls, a roaring, rushing explosion of nature that took Margaret's breath away. From Niagara, they traveled to Chicago by boat. The trip took several days, and gave Margaret her first sight of Indians, camped out along the banks of the St. Clair River. "It was twilight," she wrote, "and their blanketed forms, in listless groups or stealing along the bank with a lounge and a stride so different in its wildness from the rudeness of the white settler, gave me the first feeling that I really approached the West." Already she was beginning to feel a kind of discomfort with her fellow Americans—at least those she was meeting on the trip. "The people on the boat," she wrote, "were almost all New Englanders seeking their fortunes. They had brought with them their habits of calculation, their cautious manners, their love of polemics. . . ." It was the same unhappiness with American values that had inspired the Transcendentalist movement, the *Dial*, Brook Farm, the Temple School, the Conversations.

And her summer in the West only increased Margaret's dissatisfaction with things as they were. As the trip continued, and she began to meet Indians and to talk to them, she became increasingly angered at the treatment her countrymen were meting out to them. The Indians had about them an innate courtesy and dignity, an innate sense of beauty and respect for the land—qualities, so Margaret thought, that the white man did not even begin to appreciate. She was outraged at the arrogance with which the settlers viewed the Indians and with the cruelty and deception with which they were treated. It seemed to her they would not long be able to survive this hounding. In her journal, she wrote of the tragedy over and over again:

> Seeing the traces of the Indians who chose the most beautiful sites for their dwellings, and whose habits do not break in on that aspect of Nature under which they were born, we feel as if they were the rightful lords of a beauty they forebore to deform. But most of the settlers do not see it at all; it breathes, it speaks in vain to those who are rushing into its sphere. . . .
>
> In traveling through the country, I could not help but be struck with the force of a symbol. Wherever the hog comes, the rattlesnake disappears; the omnivorous traveler, safe in its

> stupidity, willingly and easily makes a meal of the most dangerous of reptiles, and one which the Indian looks on with a mystic awe. Even so the white settler pursues the Indian and is victor in the chase. . . .

She was disturbed, too, by what she saw of women's lives in the West—by the difficulties they faced in meeting the demands of a new way of life, and by their lack of imagination, which led them to try to copy Eastern ways instead of developing new ones. It was another demonstration to her of how little consideration society gave to women; how few opportunities it offered them; how tightly it confined them in a mold—and how deeply that treatment scarred women's minds and characters. She had just finished an article on that theme for the summer issue of the *Dial*—"The Great Lawsuit: Man vs. Men, Woman vs. Women" was its somewhat forbidding title—and everything she saw in the homes of recently transplanted Easterners only reinforced her anger at the way women were made to live.

> The great drawback upon the lives of these settlers at present is the unfitness of the women for their new lot. It has generally been the choice of the men, and the women follow as women will, doing their best for affection's sake but too often in heart-sickness and weariness. . . . [They] can rarely find any aid in domestic labor. All its various and careful tasks must often be performed, sick or well, by the mother and daughters to whom a city education has im-

parted neither the strength nor skill now demanded. . . .

With all these disadvantages for work, their resources for pleasure are fewer. When they can leave the housework, they have not learned to ride, to drive, to row alone. Their culture has too generally been that given to women to make them the "ornaments of society." They can dance but not draw; talk French, but know nothing of the language of flowers; neither in childhood were allowed to cultivate them, lest they should tan their complexions. Accustomed to the pavements of Broadway, they dare not tread the wildwood paths for fear of rattle-snakes!

Seeing much of this joylessness and inaptitude, both of body and of mind, for a lot which would be full of blessings for those prepared for it, we could not but look with deep interest on the little girls, and hope they would grow up with the strength of body, dexterity, simple tastes and resources that would fit them to enjoy and refine the Western farmer's life.

But they have a great deal to war with in the habits of thought acquired by their mothers from their own early life. . . .

If the little girls grow up strong, resolute, able to exert their faculties, their mothers mourn over their want of fashionable delicacy. Are they gay, enterprising, ready to fly about in the various ways that teach them so much, these ladies lament that "they cannot go to school, where they might learn to be quiet." They lament the want of "education" for their daughters, as if the thousand needs which call out their

> young energies, and the language of nature around, yielded no education.
>
> Their grand ambition for their children is to send them to school in some Eastern city, the measure most likely to make them useless and unhappy at home. . . . Methods copied from the education of some English Lady Augusta are as ill suited to the daughter of an Illinois farmer as satin shoes to climb the Indian mounds. An elegance she would diffuse around her, if her mind were opened to appreciate elegance; it might be of a kind new, original, enchanting, as different from that of the city belle as that of the prairie torchflower from the shopworn article that touches the cheek of that lady within her bonnet.

But with all the things that disturbed her—the obvious cruelty and contempt with which the Indians were treated; the more subtle cruelty and contempt by which women were victimized; the failure of the settlers to build a culture of their own—the West impressed Margaret, and much about it excited her.

There was, for example, the prairie—the flat, unbroken stretches of land as far as the eye could see. At first it seemed to her "to speak of the very desolation of dullness," so different was it from New England, with its mountains, valleys, and woods. But then she began to see it with new eyes, and the mystic in her responded to what she saw. ". . . I would ascend the roof of the house where we lived," she wrote while she and the Clarkes were in Chicago, "and pass many hours, needing no sight but the moon reigning in the heavens or starlight falling upon the lake, till all the lights were out in the island grove of men beneath my feet, and felt nearer heaven that there was nothing but this lovely, still reception on the earth; no towering mountains, no deep tree-shadows, nothing but plain earth and water bathed in light."

And there was the cheerful frontier roughness —the very opposite of conventional New England propriety. With all its inconveniences, it delighted the adventurer in Margaret. And she was vastly amused by those of her traveling companions who insisted on carrying the proprieties with them wherever they went. One night she and the Clarkes stayed at an inn in Pawpaw Grove, in northern Illinois, a territory they were exploring in a huge wagon—stocked with everything they would need for two weeks. The accommodations were rude at best. She and the Clarkes "partook," as she wrote, "of the miseries so often jocosely portrayed of bedchambers for twelve, a milk dish for universal handbasin, and expectations that you would use and lend your 'hankercher' for a towel. . . ." Her account continued:

> With us was a young lady who showed herself to have been bathed in the Britannic fluid . . . by the impossibility she experienced of accommodating herself to the indecorums of the scene. We ladies were to sleep in the barroom, from which its drinking visitors could be ejected only at a late hour. The outer door had no fastening to prevent their return. However, our host kindly requested we should call him if they

> did, as he had "conquered them for us" and would do so again. We had also rather hard couches (mine was the supper table); but we Yankees, born to rove, were altogether too much fatigued to stand upon trifles, and slept sweetly. . . . But I think England sat up all night, wrapped in her blanket-shawl, and with a neat lace cap upon her head—so that she would have looked perfectly the lady, if anyone had come in—shuddering and listening. I know that she was very ill the next day in requital. She watched, as her parent country watches the sea, that nobody may do wrong in any case, and deserved to have met some interruption, she was so well prepared.

And there was the wilderness—the almost virgin forests of northern Michigan and the Wisconsin territory. Toward the end of August, Margaret and the Clarkes separated for a while, and Margaret spent nine days on Mackinac Island and at Sault Sainte Marie. She wandered among the Indians—Ottawas and Chippewas—who had come to the island to receive the annual payment due them by the United States for having taken their lands, and talked with them in a gesture language she and they both understood. "There is a language of eyes and motion," she wrote, "which cannot be put into words and which teaches what words never can." At Sault Sainte Marie, she went over the rapids in a canoe paddled by her Indian guides with such exquisite skill that, as she wrote, "the silliest person would not feel afraid." In fact, the experience was a little disappointing. "Having heard such expressions used as of 'darting' or 'shooting down' the rapids, I had fancied there was a wall of rock somewhere, where descent would somehow be accomplished and that there would come some gasp of terror and delight, some sensation entirely new to me; but I found myself in smooth water before I had time to feel anything but the buoyant pleasure of being carried so lightly thru this surf amid the breakers."

By September, the trip was over and Margaret was back in Boston, conducting Conversations and reworking the section of her journal that dealt with the summer's adventures. She wanted to turn it into a book. The West was fascinating to Easterners, and there was a good chance that publication of her story would provide her with some much-needed money. Even more, there were things she wanted to say, and wanted others to hear. The West had given her a feeling about her country she had not had before. It had not changed her criticisms of American values. Indeed, it had reinforced them—given her an even stronger sense of the ugliness those values could produce. If Boston's Unitarian ministers offended her by their dull and literal-minded sermons, how much more offensive was the hypocrisy of the missionaries, who were robbing the Indians of their culture and religion and offering them in return subservience and degradation of the spirit.

But with all she had found that was ugly, her visit to the West had expanded her vision to a world beyond New England, and it had shown her that an American culture, if it was to develop, could not be a New England culture alone. The country was too big, its terrain was too diversified to permit the homogeneity of a single way of life. Even the cities in the West had a different spirit about them. Chicago and Milwaukee had a vigor that Margaret found strange and fascinating. "Had I been rich . . . I might have built a house or set up in business during my fortnight's stay at Milwaukee," she wrote, "matters move on there at so rapid a rate." That pace seemed to her to hold great promise. It met and matched the vastness of the land.

Margaret wrote the last word of her book—*Summer on the Lakes*, she called it—on her thirty-fourth birthday, May 23, 1844. It proved to be the best birthday present she could have given herself. Among its first readers, after its publication in June of that year, were two unusual New Yorkers, Ida and Horace Greeley. Horace Greeley was the publisher of the *New York Tribune*, a daily paper he had founded three years before. The *Tribune* was a crusading paper, designed "to advance the interests of the people and promote their moral, social and political well-being," and one of the causes it pressed most strongly was the cause of the American frontier: Greeley had been exhorting his readers to "go West" ever since he began publishing. *Summer on the Lakes* was bound to appeal to him. And to his wife, it was merely another example of Margaret's genius. Ida Greeley, who had lived in Boston before her marriage, had long been a passionate admirer of Margaret's. She had attended some of the earlier Conversations in Boston and, with her husband, some of the Conversations Margaret conducted at Brook Farm. Now she began pressing him to bring Margaret down to New York, install her with them in their home, and put her to work writing for his newspaper.

The idea was daring. No woman before had ever been employed as a regular writer for an American newspaper. But to Greeley, unconventionality was no drawback. On the contrary. The more he thought about his wife's idea, the more it appealed to him. He had been impressed by the Conversations, and he had read and admired some of Margaret's articles in the *Dial.* The publication of *Summer on the Lakes* tipped the balance. He would like to have Miss Fuller join his staff, as literary critic. Was she interested?

Margaret was more than interested. She was flattered and excited. It was the second demonstration in only a few months that she was finally beginning to arrive. While she was working on her book, she had needed some materials that were available only in the library. And Harvard had permitted her to use its collection—to sit in the Harvard Library to do her work. No woman previously had been allowed even to turn the knob on its doors. Greeley's offer was an even greater compliment. And it opened up possibilities that would never arise in Boston. A steady income would permit her once and for all to stop worrying about money. But even more exciting was the chance the job would give her to become truly a "public person"—to bring her ideas to the attention of an audience of fifty thousand people instead of the few hundred who read the *Dial*— or who *had* read it: its financial problems were finally defeating it, and 1844 was to be the last year of its publication.

Only one problem stood between Margaret and her acceptance of Greeley's offer: her mother. She should not be asked to live alone, with no one to depend on, and Margaret did not want to take her to New York. She loved her mother, she worried about her, she was devoted to her. But she wanted to be free of the family responsibilities she had been carrying for so long. She wanted to be on her own.

"If our family affairs could now be so arranged," she wrote her brothers, "that I might be tolerably tranquil for the next six or eight years, I should go out of life better satisfied with the page I have turned in it, than I shall if I must still toil."

Her brothers were sympathetic. Better than anyone else, they knew what a loyal daughter and sister Margaret had been, and how much of herself she had sacrificed to her family. It was time that she have her chance. Between them Arthur and Richard agreed to provide a home for Mrs. Fuller. The way was clear for Margaret to move to New York.

8

Speaking Out for Women

Margaret was expected in New York at the end of November 1844 to take up her job at the *Tribune*. The few months she had left in Boston were full of difficult and distressing tasks. The family home had to be dismantled, and her mother moved to her brother Richard's house in Cambridgeport, not far from where Margaret was born. With all her eagerness to break free, Margaret found the experience painful. "As a family we are henceforth to be parted," she wrote in her journal, the day the move was completed. "But though for months I had been preparing for this separation, the last moments were very sad." Nor was this the only separation she was facing. When she left Boston, she would be leaving a whole world—her family, her friends, the only way of life she had ever known.

For the journey she was about to make was far longer than the distance that separated Boston from New York. The two were very different cities, and stood for very different things. Boston was the cultural and intellectual center of the country—the Athens of America, its citizens called it, and to them it was the *only* city. New York was the largest city in the country, the commercial and financial center where over a quarter of a million people made their homes. The two cities were of an age—both had been founded a little more than two hundred years before—but Boston seemed, somehow, much older, more settled, less brash. With all its history, there was something vulgar and upstart about New York—at least, so most Bostonians felt. For Margaret, with all her intellectual and cultural interests, to desert the *Dial* and the Conversations—those quintessentially Bostonian institutions—to write for a New York newspaper was, to many of her friends, just short of selling her soul. Emerson was forced to admit that journalism was honorable work. "Still," he said, "this employment is not satisfactory to me."

Margaret knew how sharp a break she was making. Much more was involved, she realized, than merely changing her residence and her means of livelihood. "I shall feel my separation from almost all that has been companionable to me," she wrote Waldo. But no expectation of homesickness could dissuade her from her plans. She knew she was doing the right thing. In many ways, she had never been a true New Englander. Her intensity and her self-assertiveness were as un-Bostonian as they were "unfeminine"; her extravagances of feeling—her headaches, her depressions, her preoccupation with the darker, mysterious side of life—were out of place and "odd." Her Boston friends loved Margaret, but she was sometimes a bit of an embarrassment to them. And Margaret loved her Boston friends, but she sometimes wanted to shake them for their almost smug self-righteousness.

More important, there was her sense of mission, her sense that she had been born to leave her mark on the world. Neither the work she had done so far nor the recognition she had received lived up to her estimate of her abilities. The "mountainous me" in Margaret, of which Emerson spoke, aspired to mountain heights, and she was afraid she would never be able to scale them if she remained in the closed and somewhat precious world of Boston Transcendentalism.

Moreover, Margaret knew that if she was to leave her mark on the world, she needed the discipline to work in an orderly fashion—to meet deadlines, and not postpone them; to write on assignment, not inspiration; to work on one project at a time, instead of darting from one to another. The demands of a regular, daily job would impose a schedule on her and sharpen her craftsmanship as a writer. Conversation would always remain her first love. But writing was the skill she must cultivate if she was to speak to the world, and New York was the place where she could pursue it.

She had one more task to complete before she began her new life. She wanted to revise and expand the piece on women she had written for the previous summer's *Dial*, and to publish it as a short book. That piece meant a great deal to her: if her responsibilities to her family and the restrictions of life in Boston had kept her from the recognition she believed she deserved, how much more tightly was she hemmed in by the simple fact of her sex! She wanted to tell as much of the world as would listen that women deserved better, richer lives than they usually led.

But when she sat down to begin work, she found she could not. She was too tormented by the emotional strain of leaving her old life. She was depressed almost to desperation, her demons had almost full possession of her, and her headaches were more blinding and frequent than usual. She had a terrible fear that she would never again be herself—that she would never get to New York, that she would never be strong enough to take up her new job.

Her friend Caroline Sturgis rescued her from her misery, proposing that the two of them take a vacation at the quiet Hudson River village of Fishkill. There Margaret could relax, regain her strength, and work, when she was ready, in an atmosphere of calm and peace.

The vacation proved to be just the medicine Margaret needed. Away from everything and everyone—save Caroline—she found herself, as if by a miracle, able to work again. And work she did, not only revising and rewriting the article, but reading voraciously.

The manuscript was finished on November 15. Margaret was pleased with it. Of all the things she had ever written, it was the closest to her own feelings and her own experiences. The problems it talked about were problems she knew intimately. But at the same time she was talking for herself, she was also talking for other women. She described the satisfaction she felt in a letter to William Henry Channing, just two days after she had written the final word.

> At last, my dear William, I have finished the pamphlet. The last day it kept spinning out beneath my hand. After taking a long walk early on one of the noble, exhilarating sort of mornings, I sat down to write and did not put the last stroke till nine in the evening. Then I felt a delightful glow as if I had put a good deal of my true life in it, as if, suppose I went away now, the measure of my footprint would be left on the earth.

Margaret wanted to call the book by the same long and forbidding title as the *Dial* article. Fortunately, however, Caroline was able to dissuade her, and when she turned the manuscript over to Horace Greeley, who was publishing it, it bore the simple title, *Woman in the Nineteenth Century.*

It was an extraordinary work. Nothing like it had appeared in the United States before. Indeed, only one book in the same vein had ever been published anywhere. And that was fifty years earlier, in

England, when Mary Wollstonecraft's *Vindication of the Rights of Woman* had appeared. But although both books were pleas for women's rights, there were important differences between them. The British book was written under the influence of the ideas that had sparked the American and French revolutions—the ideas of innate human rights and of political democracy. Margaret was concerned with social roles and personal relationships—with women's right to choose their own ways of life and their own occupations, and with their right to full social equality with men.

She was not, of course, alone in her concern for women. There were other feminists in the United States and a small group of them were actively campaigning—often against deep and bitter resistance—for a number of specific reforms that would improve women's lives. Eliza Farnham and Lydia Maria Child were writing and speaking out against laws that deprived women of the right to hold property—reducing them to the status of chattel; and against court rulings that upheld a husband's right to abuse and even beat his wife. Lucretia Mott and Elizabeth Cady Stanton were proclaiming the heretical doctrine that women had as much right to the ballot as men.

Margaret's demands were broader, grander, more overarching. She called for nothing less than a social, ethical, and psychological revolution—a revolution in the ways people lived their lives, both as individuals and as husband and wives; a revolution in the ways men and women saw themselves and one another; a revolution that would finally acknowledge women's right to determine their own lives:

We would have every arbitrary barrier thrown down. We would have every path laid open to Woman as fully as to Man. Were this done and a slight temporary fermentation allowed to subside, we should see crystallizations more pure and of more various beauty. We believe the divine energy would pervade nature to a degree unknown in the history of former ages, and that no discordant collision but a ravishing harmony of the spheres would ensue.

Yet then and only then will mankind be ripe for this, when inward and outward freedom for Woman as much as for Man shall be acknowledged as a *right*, not yielded as a concession. As the friend of the Negro assumes that one man cannot by right hold another in bondage, so should the friend of Woman assume that Man cannot by right lay even well-meant restrictions on Woman. If the Negro be a soul; if the woman be a soul, apparelled in flesh, to one Master only are they accountable. There is but one law for souls, and if there is to be an interpreter of it, he must come not as man or son of man, but as son of God.

Were thought and feeling once so far elevated that Man should esteem himself the brother and friend, but nowise the lord and master, of Woman—were he really bound with her in equal worship—arrangements as to function and employment would be of no consequence. What Woman needs is not as a woman to act or rule, but as a nature to grow, as an intellect to discern, as a soul to live freely and unimpeded to unfold such powers as were given her when we left our common home.

Nor would women be the only beneficiaries if Margaret's revolution was accomplished. Men would benefit, too:

> . . . I mean both men and women; these are the two halves of one thought. I lay no special stress on the welfare of either. I believe that the development of one cannot be effected without that of the other. My highest wish is that this truth should be distinctly and rationally apprehended, and the conditions of life and freedom recognized as the same for the daughters and the sons of time; twin exponents of a divine thought.

For as long as women continued to be treated as men's inferiors, Margaret pointed out, marriage would be demeaned:

> It is idle to speak of nations where polygamy is an institution or seraglios a custom, while practices far more debasing haunt, well-nigh fill, every city and every town, and so far as union of one with one is believed to be the only pure form of marriage, a great majority of societies and individuals are still doubtful whether the earthly bond must be a meeting of souls, or only supposes a contract of convenience and utility. Were Woman established in the rights of an immortal being, this could not be. She would not . . . be perverted by the current of opinion that seizes her, into the belief that she must marry, if it be only to find a protector and a home of her own. Neither would Man,

> if he thought the connection of permanent importance, form it so lightly. . . . Were he a step higher he would not carelessly enter into a relation where he might not be able to do the duty of a friend, as well as a protector from external ill, to the other party. . . .

And worst of all, women, by viewing themselves as men viewed them, were losing their character. Tricked into believing they had no value save the value men were willing to give them, they lost their faith in themselves as persons and gave themselves over to vanity and selfishness, so they could not even recognize the sisterhood of their sex, and help one another. Margaret wrote:

> A little while since, I was at one of the most fashionable places of public resort. I saw there many women, dressed without regard to the season or the demands of the place in apery, or as it looked, in mockery of European fashion. I saw their eyes restlessly courting attention. I saw the way in which it was paid: the style of devotion, almost an open sneer, which it pleased those ladies to receive from men whose expression marked their own position in the moral and intellectual world. Those women went to their pillows with their heads full of folly, their hearts of jealousy or gratified vanity; those men, with the low opinion they already entertained of Woman confirmed. These were American *ladies*; that is, they were of that class who have wealth and leisure to make full use of the days and confer benefits on others. . . .

> Soon after I met a circle of women stamped by society as among the most degraded of their sex. "How," it was asked of them, "did you come here?" for by the society that I saw in the former place they were shut up in a prison. The causes were not difficult to trace: love of dress, love of flattery, love of excitement. They had not dresses like the other ladies, so they stole them; they could not pay for flattery by distinctions and the dower of a worldly marriage, so they paid by the profanations of their persons. In excitement, more and more madly from day to day, they drowned the voice of conscience.
>
> Now I ask you, my sisters, if the women at the fashionable house be not answerable for those women being kept in the prison?

Throughout the book, Margaret gave evidence of her courage—in discussing, for example, topics like prostitution, which were taboo among respectable people. She gave evidence of her staggering scholarship—in the example after example she offered of real and fictional women whose lives and works belied the myth of feminine inferiority. And she gave evidence of the ideal she had always kept before her—the ideal of translating the demands of abstract morality into concrete terms, and turning the what-should-be into what actually was. "I think women need, especially at this juncture, a much greater range of occupations than they have, to rouse their latent powers. . . . In families that I know, some girls like to saw wood, others to use carpenters' tools. Where these tastes are indulged, cheerfulness and good humor are promoted. Where they are forbidden, because 'such things are not proper for girls,' they grow sullen and mischievous."

Finally, Margaret called on women to learn to act independently of men:

"That her hand may be given with dignity," she wrote, "she must be able to stand alone. . . . I have urged on Woman independence of Man, not that I do not think the sexes mutually needed by one another, but because in Woman this fact has led to an excessive devotion which has cooled love, degraded marriage, and prevented either sex from being what it should be to itself or the other. . . ."

And she urged women to take their emancipation into their own hands. "I believe that at present women are the best helpers of one another," she wrote. "Let them think, let them act, let them know what they need. We only ask of men to remove arbitrary barriers."

Once those barriers were removed, the world might not even appear to have changed very much:

> I have no doubt that a large proportion of women would give themselves to the same employments as now. . . . Mothers will delight to make the nest soft and warm. Nature will take care of that, no need to clip the wings of any bird that wants to soar and sing, or find in itself the strength of pinion for a migratory flight unusual to its kind. The difference would be that *all* need not be constrained to employments for which *some* are unfit. . . .

> It is not Woman, but the law of right, the law of growth that speaks in us and demands the perfection of each being in its kind—apple as apple, Woman as Woman . . . what concerns me now is that my life be a beautiful, powerful, in a word, a complete life in its kind.

Woman in the Nineteenth Century came off the press in February 1845, shortly after Margaret moved to New York. A few courageous critics praised it; many more damned the book and its author. It was immoral and irreligious. She was wanton and quite mad. But praised or damned, the book was noticed. Copies found their way to nearly every American city and even to Europe; the first edition was sold out within a week. No longer was Margaret merely a Boston phenomenon, the archetype of those peculiar, intellectual women. She was a public figure, a power to be reckoned with.

9

The Journalist

Margaret's first article for the *Tribune* appeared on December 1, 1844, only a week after her arrival in New York. Its subject was a book by Emerson—his second series of essays, which she had read when she was in Fishkill with Caroline. To Margaret, the essays reflected everything that was good and everything that was bad about Boston and her old life, and about her old friend Waldo.

The good, of course, was in the idealism that the Transcendentalists embodied, and their desire to ennoble themselves and their society. "If only as a representative of the claims of individual culture in a nation which tends to lay such stress on artificial organization and external results," Margaret wrote, "Mr. Emerson would be invaluable here. History will inscribe his name as a father of the country, for he is one who pleads her cause against herself."

The bad was the bloodlessness, the calm, the want of passion. "Here is undoubtedly the man of ideas," she wrote, "but we want the ideal man also; want the heart and genius of human life to interpret it, and here our satisfaction is not so perfect. We doubt this friend raised himself too early to the perpendicular and did not lie along the ground long enough to hear the secret whispers of our parent life. We could wish he might be thrown by conflicts on the lap of mother earth, to see if he would not rise again with added powers."

In her criticism, Margaret had always been direct and outspoken. She never pussyfooted, even for her closest friends, and she always had a sharp eye for the second-rate. That integrity and tough-mindedness were even more visible in the work she did for the *Tribune*. In part, it was the result of deadline pressure. Margaret was supposed to write three critical articles a week for the paper, and that left her little time for flourishes or gingerly pirouettes, even if she had wanted to include them. In part, it was her subject matter. Many of the books she wrote about were ones she herself would previously never have read—much less reviewed. They were popular works, with no aspirations to immortality, and the very act of reading and writing about them forced Margaret to clarify her own criteria and to sharpen her insights and understanding. She became much less tolerant of the precious and pretentious and much more appreciative of the modest and straightforward. "I have never regarded literature merely as a collection of exquisite products, but rather as a means of mutual interpretation," she wrote. And by that standard, many works her Boston friends treated condescendingly seemed to her to merit serious critical attention. At the same time, she had no hesitation in condemning works which they regarded highly. She did not think very much of Longfellow or of James Russell Lowell, and she said so. Nor were her judgments influenced by her vanity. She was full of praise for Edgar Allan Poe, who had said some harsh and unflattering things about her and her book in his review of *Woman in the Nineteenth Century.*

But probably the most important cause for the change in Margaret's writing was the change that was occurring in Margaret herself. She was no longer a protected, provincial gentlewoman. She had traveled; she had seen something of her country and its people. And she was independent—a working woman in a busy commercial city. Literature was still her first love and idealism her first value, and she still would certainly have described herself as a Transcendentalist. But increasingly, real people and real problems were becoming her concern. She was beginning to see that more was required to solve the real problems of real people than merely quickening the soul and working from within outward.

In her Boston days, she had little faith in social action of any sort. She had never, for example, been active in the Abolitionist movement. Though slavery appalled her, it was an evil she knew about only in the abstract—it was not part of her daily life; she did not see it around her. But now, in New York, when she saw evil with her own eyes, she spoke out sharply against it, as she had spoken out against the treatment of the Indians in *Summer on the Lakes*, and as she did, in *Woman in the Nineteenth Century*, in her defense of "fallen" women.

That defense had grown directly out of personal experience. When she and Caroline were at Fishkill, she had gone to visit Sing Sing, the prison at Ossining, a few miles down the river. Sing Sing had a special section for women, most of whom had been imprisoned for petty theft and prostitution. It was under the direction of a matron unusual in her humanity and decency—a woman who, unlike the usual run of prison personnel, did not think of herself as a zookeeper, and who wanted to help her prisoners rather than punish them. When Margaret asked if she could talk with the prisoners, the matron was delighted. The visit made an enormous impression on Margaret, and she wrote in her journal,

> These women were among the so-called worst, and all from the lowest haunts of vice. Yet nothing could have been more decorous than their conduct, while it was also frank, and they showed a sensibility and a sense of propriety which would not have disgraced any society. All passed, indeed, much as in my Boston classes. I told them I was writing about Woman; and as my path had been a favored one, I wanted to gain information from those who had been tempted and afflicted. They seemed to reply in the same spirit in which I asked. Several, how-

> ever, expressed a wish to see me alone, as they could then say all, which they could not bear to do before another. I shall go there again, and take time for this. It is very gratifying to see the influence these few months of gentle and intelligent treatment have had upon these women: indeed, it is wonderful.

Margaret was true to her word. She had told the women she would visit with them on Christmas, and she did, spending her first holiday in New York at Sing Sing. And she took a special interest in the women prisoners at Blackwell's Island, not far from the Greeleys' home.

"Seven hundred females are confined in the Penitentiary opposite this point," Margaret wrote, shortly after she had arrived in the city. "We can pass over in a boat in a few minutes. I mean to visit, to talk and read with them." Her interest and her concern continued, and she tried to keep up her relationship with several of the women after their discharge from prison, sometimes inviting them to stay for a while at the Greeleys' before they took up their new lives.

But she soon realized that her personal intervention and example, no matter how encouraging, were hardly an answer to the problems the women faced. Social action was needed—and not only on behalf of "fallen" women, but on behalf of the thousands of other New Yorkers who had no resources of their own and who were dependent on society to make their lives tolerable. The city had institutions designed, presumably, to help these people—there were homes for orphans, for the aged, for the poor, for the blind, and for the deaf; there were hospitals for the physically ill and asylums for the mentally disturbed. Together with William Henry Channing, she made visits to several of these places and, in the middle of March, the *Tribune* published her report on the conditions she had found. It was blistering: the institutions were merely dumping grounds, and Margaret said so.

In all, she wrote six pieces exposing the nightmares of the city's so-called charities, urging support for efforts to improve them, and suggesting that halfway houses be created for men and women on their way back to life in the outside world.

Greeley was delighted with Margaret's campaigns—they satisfied both his crusader's instinct to do good and his businessman's desire to sell as many papers as he could. Whatever fears he might have had about his daring experiment in hiring a woman—and a Boston intellectual, at that—were quickly put to rest. Margaret was one of the *Tribune*'s major attractions. It was customary at the time not to sign newspaper pieces, but the new author was identified by an asterisk, and it took very little time for her readers to figure out that "*" was in fact Margaret Fuller.

But Greeley did have his complaints about his new staff member. She usually turned out her required three columns a week, but it was often difficult for her, and she made that quite clear. She still had her headaches, her nervous anxieties, her exhaustions, and he was intolerant of them: they came, he was sure, from her predilection for tea and coffee, neither of which he drank. And she didn't like working downtown at the newspaper's office on Nassau Street. He found that both infuriating and incomprehensible. He had printer's ink in his veins and, were it not for his wife and infant son, would have been entirely content to spend twenty-four hours a day at the *Tribune*. But Margaret much preferred writing in her room at the Greeleys' house at Turtle Bay, on the East River near Fiftieth Street. It was in the city, but not of it, and it gave her the peace and quiet she needed to do her work. In a letter to a friend, she wrote of it almost lyrically:

> This place, is to me, entirely charming. It is so completely in the country, and all around is so bold and free. It is two miles or more from the thickly settled parts of New York, but omnibusses and cars give me constant access to the city, and while I can readily see what and whom I will, I can command time and retirement. Stopping on the Harlem Road, you enter a lane nearly a quarter of a mile long, and going by a small brook and pond that lock in the place and ascending a slightly rising ground, get sight of the house, which, old-fashioned and of a mellow tint, fronts on a flower-garden filled with shrubs, large vines and trim box borders. On both sides of the house are beautiful trees, standing fair, full-grown and clear. Passing through a wide hall, you come out upon a piazza stretching the whole length of the house, where one can walk in all weathers; and

> thence, by a step or two, on a lawn, with picturesque masses of rocks, shrubs, and trees overlooking the East River. Gravel paths lead by several turns down the steep bank to the water's edge, where, round the rocky point, a small bay curves, in which boats are lying, and owing to the current and the set of the tide, the sails glide sidelong, seeming to greet the house as they sweep by. The beauty here, seen by moonlight, is truly transporting.

Margaret had another reason for wanting to work at home, when she could. She was in love, and the atmosphere of the crowded, noisy *Tribune* office clashed violently with her mood. On New Year's Eve, just a month after she arrived in New York, the Greeleys gave a party. One of the guests was James Nathan, a man about Margaret's age who had come to the United States from Germany and had overcome poverty to become successful in the commission business. Nathan was immediately attracted to Margaret by her "high intellectuality, purity of sentiment and winning conversation," as he put it—and probably also by her reputation and near-fame. Margaret found him "gentle and civilized," and was enchanted by his German origin—she had long been a devotee of German culture and German literature—and by his blue eyes. And she was especially drawn to him because he was Jewish. She had never before met any Jews, and she had recently had an almost mystic presentiment that she soon would.

A few weeks after they met, and just about the same time that *Woman in the Nineteenth Century* was published, Nathan invited Margaret to go with him to see a plaster model of Jerusalem, then on exhibit in New York. Margaret accepted his invitation with a tantalizing sense of destiny: she had planned to visit the exhibit with another friend and, at the last moment, had changed her mind.

The appointment confirmed all her hopes for it. Nathan was bright, he was gallant; his conversation and his interests showed that "kernel of nobleness" that Margaret was always looking for. And he hinted of tragedy and unfulfilled longings in his life, of regrets and blighted hopes. The mystery itself attracted her, evoking all her need to be a confidante. They went to concerts together; she gave him a copy of *Woman* and, because they were both busy people with relatively little free time, they sent notes back and forth to each other—often several times a day.

But something more than their crowded schedules kept them from seeing each other as often as they would have liked. The Greeleys did not quite approve of the relationship. They were not sure that Nathan was a suitable companion for Margaret, and though they agreed in principle with Margaret's demands for independence for women, she was after all a maiden lady of thirty-four and they were responsible for her as long as she lived at their house. So Margaret did not feel free to see Nathan either at the *Tribune* office or at the Greeleys'. Instead, they met on the street, or at the homes of friends Margaret had known before she came to New York.

One of these was Christopher Cranch—a poet and an old friend from Transcendentalist days. "Should you like to go with me on Monday evening to hear the Messiah?" Margaret wrote Nathan shortly after they had visited the Jerusalem exhibit. "If so, will you come to tea to Mr. Cranch's at six or a little later and take me?"

And, only a few days thereafter: "Are you very busy? If not, walk up through John Street towards the Doctor's about twenty minutes past ten. But if you are busy, don't disturb yourself. I go that way at any rate."

But outside problems—their busy schedules, the Greeleys' disapproval—were not the only ones Margaret and Nathan faced. Almost from the beginning, there were difficulties between them. Margaret could not admit it even to herself, but Nathan was, essentially, a rather ordinary, conventional man. And she did not conform to his expectations of what was feminine. There was her reserve—the difficulty she had in confiding her deepest feelings to anyone else while she was at the same time eager to hear their confidences, and to play mother confessor. Almost from the moment they met, Nathan was telling her the story of his life, and confiding in her about his problems, his feelings, and his ambitions: he was calling forth her sympathy and understanding. Although he demanded that she confide in him in return, she could not do it—not yet, at least. It was simply not in her character. Their first quarrel came on this count, no more than a month after they had begun to see one another. And it was Margaret who healed the breach. "It would be more generous to be more confiding," she wrote him, "but

I cannot. You must see me as I am. . . . Our education and relations are so different—and those of each as yet scarce known to the other—slight misunderstandings may arise. . . ."

The second quarrel, less than two weeks later, was far more serious. Nathan could not understand that Margaret's intensity of style and her directness in expressing her affection were just that—and nothing more; not acts of coquetry or seduction, not invitations to physical intimacy. Long before Margaret felt ready, he made a sexual approach to her. She was heartsick. "Yesterday was, perhaps," she wrote him, "a sadder day than I had in all my life. It did not seem to me an act of 'Providence,' but of some ill demon, that had exposed me to what was to every worthy and womanly feeling so humiliating. Neither could I reconcile myself to your having such thoughts, and just when you had induced me to trust you so absolutely."

This time it was Nathan's turn to mend the quarrel. He did: his note of apology arrived at the Greeleys' while Margaret was still writing her angry and disappointed letter to him. "I have your note," she wrote. ". . . You have said there is in yourself both a lower and a higher than I was aware of. Since you said this, I suppose I have seen that lower! It is—is it not? the man of the world, as you said you see 'the dame' in me. Yet shall we not both rise above it? I feel as if I could now, and in that faith, say to you, dear friend—kill me with truth, if it be needed, but never give me less. . . . Wilt thou not come with me before God and promise me severe truth, and patient tenderness, that will never, if it can be avoided, misinterpret the impulses of my soul. I am willing you should see them just as they are, but I am not willing for the reaction from the angelic view to that of the man of the world. Yet that time is past when I could protect myself by reserve. I must now seem just as I feel, and you must protect me. Are you equal to this? Will an unfailing reverent love shelter the 'sister of your soul?' If so, we may yet be happy together some few hours, and our parting be sad but not bitter."

For that parting, as Margaret knew, was not far off. It was now March, and Nathan had been scheduled for a long time to leave in May for an extended business trip to Europe. Margaret persuaded him to postpone his departure until June, but even that gave them only a little over two months together. During that time, the romance became a fire storm. They saw each other as often as possible; they wrote to each other whenever they had a moment to spare. They quarreled; they reconciled. She sent him books; he sent her his Newfoundland puppy, Josey. He continued to pour out his heart to her, to acknowledge his sins and his deficiencies; to spin out his dreams and aspirations. He talked of a "new and greater religion," of a "vital energy," of "spirit identity." And the more he showed himself and his feelings to her, the more he evoked her warmth, her trust, her loyalty, her dependence. Her letters to him became hymns of adoration. She called him "*Mein Liebster,*" "loved soul," "dearest." The difference in their religions made marriage between them an unlikely prospect. But Margaret had long since lost any real interest in marriage. Her age, her public status, and her habit of independence—all of these would have made it difficult for her to fit herself into a conventional pattern of married life. Still, she wanted and needed someone she could love and lean on, and trust. And by the time Nathan left for Germany, that was the role he filled. He had become the emotional center of her life—the person who touched her most closely and who spoke most intimately to her hopes and her needs.

10

The Dream: Europe

No specific date had been set for Nathan's return from Europe. He might be gone a year or more. He had considerable business to attend to, which might take him all the way to the Near East, and he hoped to visit for a while with his mother in Hamburg. So his and Margaret's friendship depended now on letters—and on the memories they kept of each other.

On her side, Margaret did everything she could to keep the friendship alive. She wrote Nathan often—long, intimate, detailed letters—and she thought about him even more often. Daily, her memories of the time they had spent together were rekindled by some sight they had both seen, some person with whom they had both talked. She was quick to respond to the favors he asked of her. She prevailed on her old friend George Bancroft, a Bostonian who had just been appointed Secretary of the Navy, to write a letter of introduction for Nathan to American officials abroad. She made arrangements with Greeley to have some of Nathan's travel notes published in the *Tribune*. She had no idea when—or if—she and Nathan would ever see each other again, but that did not change her feeling for him. He was now her alter ego, the emotional center and core of her life. Present or absent, he was always with her.

Nathan was far less constant. Perhaps it was more difficult for him to keep his memories and her image vivid in his mind. Perhaps he simply did not have the faculty. Perhaps his business and his travels, the new sights and new acquaintances, were too great a distraction. He was, as he himself had told Margaret, a man of the world. Perhaps Margaret had never meant as much to him as he did to her, perhaps he had less need for such a close relationship. In any event, although his letters to her were warm and affectionate, they were far shorter than hers, and came less frequently. She wrote him four or five letters for every one he wrote to her. She was disappointed, but not disillusioned. She had absolute confidence in him.

The early days of his absence were made easier for her by a visit from her mother, in mid-June. Margaret was delighted to see her, and much enjoyed taking her sight-seeing and introducing her around. Then, in August, Emerson came down to visit for a few days, "full of free talk and in serene beauty as ever," as she wrote Nathan. And in October, Margaret took a vacation, and went up to Boston to visit for a month.

When she returned to New York, she did not go back to the Greeleys' home, but took a room for herself in a boardinghouse in downtown Manhattan. For quite a while she had not been entirely happy at her employer's home. She had always been distressed by Ida Greeley's housekeeping: Margaret was fastidious; Ida, casual. And Horace Greeley was a food faddist. Over his protests, Margaret continued to indulge her taste for coffee and tea. But his idiosyncrasies of diet made the Greeleys' table a frugal one: the dinner was usually austere, and the dinner hour did not encourage animated conversation. In addition Margaret's relationship with Nathan had opened up a difference between her and the Greeleys that could not be easily bridged. They did not really like Nathan or approve of the relationship, and his departure for Europe could not heal the rift that had developed. She and the Greeleys were still friends. But all of them knew that they would be better friends if they did not live together. Besides, Margaret had been in New York for nearly a year now, and was entirely able to cope with the city on her own. The only drawback to the new arrangement was financial—living would now be more expensive for Margaret. But Greeley was so pleased with her work for the paper that he was planning to increase her salary, so she would have additional money coming in.

Then, at the end of February, there came a chance for Margaret to fulfill her oldest and most precious dream. Although she had not made many close friends in New York, she had met one couple, Marcus and Rebecca Spring, whom she very much liked. The Springs were Quakers and deeply involved in social reform. Marcus, a wealthy merchant, was a Fourierist. He had been one of the first to purchase shares in Brook Farm and was active in the affairs of the North American Phalanx, a Fourierist colony in New Jersey. Rebecca was one of the most devoted supporters of Margaret's efforts to help women newly released from prison. The Springs had one child, a bright and active little boy named Eddie, who was as fond of Margaret as his parents were, and who often brought roses to her at her office at the *Tribune*. Eddie was one of Margaret's great joys in the city. She had always loved children, and Eddie Spring was a particularly lively and responsive youngster. For a long time, the Springs had been planning to make an extended tour of Europe, starting in the summer of 1846, and now they asked Margaret if she would join them, traveling with them for at least a year, at their expense. To help her to accept the gift without embarrassment, they called on Eddie's love and admiration for her: he would enjoy the trip far more with Miss Fuller there to tutor him and to help him appreciate the new world he would be discovering. Or, if she preferred, Margaret could consider the money merely a loan, to be repaid out of the royalties of *Woman in the Nineteenth Century*, which was soon to be published in England and which might, in time, earn Margaret enough in royalties to pay them back.

No proposal could have excited Margaret more.

Europe had been her goal ever since she was a child and had read of its ancient glories, and one of her deepest disappointments was that she did not seem, as the years went by, to come any closer to attaining it. And that meant that some part of herself seemed always to be beyond her grasp. For Margaret's yearning for Europe had in it much more than the usual tourist impulse. She had always had a strong sense that she belonged in Europe, that it would feel like home to her—that her journey across the Atlantic would be a return, not a departure. She loved her own country and had great hopes for it. Her roots were deep in New England soil: her ancestor Thomas Fuller had immigrated to the Massachusetts Bay Colony in 1638. But a great piece of Margaret was European. She sensed that the intensity and passion that caused her so much trouble in America would be much more congenial to Europeans.

But she could not afford the indulgence of a trip purely for pleasure, nor imagine being paid as a tutor to Eddie Spring. The arrangements she had made with Greeley for the publication of Nathan's travel notes gave her an idea. If it was agreeable to Greeley, she would take a year's leave of absence from her regular duties at the *Tribune*, and write pieces for the paper while she was abroad, reporting to Americans on people and events of particular interest. Greeley had no objections, and the conclusion of these arrangements made Margaret America's first foreign correspondent. No one before had ever performed such a function.

The Springs and Margaret were to leave from

Boston at the beginning of August, and Margaret planned to leave the *Tribune* about a month before, so that she could take a short vacation and say good-by to her friends and family in Massachusetts. For the time she remained in New York, she was constantly busy, writing her columns for the paper and preparing a group of her essays and critical articles for publication in book form. She had written Nathan about her trip almost the moment the plans were made, but he did not reply to her letter—or the several that followed—until some time in June. He expected his travels to take him to London by September, he told her, and that coincided with the Springs' itinerary. He and Margaret planned to meet there—or, if he could not make it, he would leave a message, proposing another time to meet, at the office of his friend, Mr. Delf, who was the agent for an American publishing firm in England. Margaret more than looked forward to the reunion. It was over a year since she and Nathan had seen each other. Nothing could have persuaded her not to make the trip to Europe, but the discovery that Nathan was returning to New York would have put her in serious conflict. She did not have to face that conflict. Nathan would be in Europe.

By prearrangement with Greeley, Margaret's "Farewell to New York"—her last piece for the *Tribune* as a writer on the domestic scene—appeared on August 1, the day she and the Springs sailed for Europe. It was warm in its praise of the city, where, Margaret wrote, "twenty months have presented me with a richer and more varied exercise for thought and life, than twenty years could in any other part of these United States." And it expressed her hope for the country—the ideal America she had dreamed of ever since her Boston days:

> I go to behold the wonders of art, and the temples of old religion. But I shall see no forms of beauty and majesty beyond what my country is capable of producing in myriad variety, if she has but the soul to will it; no temple to compare with what she might erect in the ages; if the catchword of the time, a sense of *divine order*, should become no more a mere word of form, but a deeply-rooted and pregnant idea in her life.

And why should she not have hope that her country would in time realize her dream for it? She was, after all, finally beginning to realize her dream for herself.

II

The Grand Tour

Margaret and the Springs sailed on the *Cambria*, one of the first ocean liners to be powered by steam as well as sail. Its engines and the calm waters collaborated to speed the trip, and it set a transatlantic record by making the crossing to Liverpool in only ten and a half days. It was ten and a half days too long for Margaret. She was sickened by the sound and smell of the machinery, and she hated the constant sense that the floor might begin to heave beneath her feet at any moment. Her head ached, her stomach felt queasy, and no matter how hard she tried, she could not rid herself of a sense of foreboding. The ocean seemed to her an enemy—threatening, treacherous, alien. "In the evening," she wrote, "when the wind was favorable and the sails set, so that the vessel looked like a great winged creature darting across the apparently measureless expanse, the effect was very grand, but ah! for such a spectacle one pays too dearly. I far prefer looking out upon the 'blue and foaming sea' from a safe shore."

But the voyage was finally over, and the real journey began. England and Scotland were first, with their "wonders of art and temples of old religion"—the relics of the early Roman invaders, the ruined castles, the centuries-old cathedrals, the masterpieces at the National and Dulwich Galleries—all of them just as she had imagined.

The people were a different matter. They were creatures of time—a fact she had not always bothered to remember—and they did not always look as she had pictured them. Thomas De Quincey, for example, whom she met in Edinburgh, was now in his sixties, and often somewhat addled—possibly as a result of the early addiction to opium he had described in *Confessions of an English Opium-Eater*. He was not always lucid, and the past was frequently more real to him than the present. For most of the time Margaret spent with him, he was in good spirits and in command of himself—articulate and urbane. But a far cry from the man who, years before, had shocked her and his other readers with his descriptions of the ghastly visions he had under the influence of the drug, which had originally been prescribed for him as a pain-killer.

Even more surprising was William Wordsworth, England's Poet Laureate, whom Margaret visited at his home in the Lake Country. Wordsworth's age—

he was now seventy-six—had not dimmed his mind. But to Margaret he had always been an eternal youth—the poet of romance and of nature—and she was not prepared for what she saw. "No Apollo flaming with youthful glory," she wrote to the *Tribune*, "laurel-crowned and lyre in hand, but instead a reverend old man, clothed in black and walking with cautious step along the level garden path."

But the really bizarre reminder of man's mortality came in London, at the home of a physician, Southwood Smith. Smith had been a friend of the political philosopher Jeremy Bentham, who had died fourteen years before and had directed in his will that his body be given to Smith for dissection and his skeleton preserved. Nor was this merely a tasteless joke. It was Bentham's statement of his belief in science and his desire to help its advance. The prejudice against dissection was strong and Bentham had hoped that through this dramatic act he could help overcome it.

Margaret had expected to be revolted at the sight of the skeleton. But she found she was not. Smith had dressed it up to resemble the flesh-and-blood man who had once covered it, and had seated it on a chair in his study. It was, Margaret wrote, "dressed in the same dress he habitually wore, stuffed out to be an exact resemblance of life, and with a portrait mask in wax, the best I ever saw. . . . The figure leans a little forward, resting the hands on a stick which Bentham had always carried, and had named 'Dapple'; the attitude is quite easy, the expression of the whole quite mild, winning, yet highly individual."

And Margaret also treated her readers to an

account of her meeting with Thomas Carlyle, one of the towering literary figures of the time, who had been among her early heroes. Carlyle, too, was different from the picture her imagination had first drawn of him, but in this case she was not surprised. She had seen the change in his point of view over the years, from his early admiration for Goethe and his commitment to freedom to the cynicism that permeated his book, *On Heroes, Hero-Worship, and the Heroic in History.* So she was prepared to disagree with him. But she had practically no chance to. As she wrote for the *Tribune*:

> He does not converse—only harangues. . . . Carlyle allows no one a chance, but bears down all opposition, not only by his wit and onset of words, resistless in their sharpness as so many bayonets, but by actual physical superiority, raising his voice and rushing on his opponent with a torrent of sound . . . You do not love him, perhaps, nor revere, and perhaps, also, he would only laugh at you if you did; but you like him heartily . . . and you cannot see him without the most hearty refreshment and good-will, for he is original, rich, and strong enough to afford a thousand faults. . . .

Reports on people and places were standard for a traveling writer, and Margaret produced them in abundance. But her dispatches contained more than this standard fare. She now thought in social and political terms—terms very different from the aesthetic abstractions that had preoccupied her when she lived in Boston. More and more she cared about people, about the ways they lived and the ways society controlled their lives, depriving many of them of even the simplest necessities. She could not ignore the signs she saw all around her in Britain's cities of the contrast between wealth and poverty; she could not ignore the evidence of the misery in which most people lived.

That misery was in large part the result of the Industrial Revolution, which was tearing through Britain like a hurricane. Men, women, and children by the thousands labored in the mills and factories for long hours at starvation wages; filth, noise, and ugliness were all around them. And for thousands of others, there was no work to be had—machines had taken their places. Efforts at social reform were under way: there were campaigns for the improvement of working conditions and programs—some of them successful—for the establishment of evening schools and libraries to give people at least the rudiments of an education. Writers like Charles Dickens were producing books that were, as much as anything else, pleas for social action. But progress was slow, and the situation was desperate. Margaret could see it in the faces of the beggars who crowded the streets—demanding money, pleading and whining for it, fighting wildly with one another for any coin a passerby might toss. She could see it, too, in the faces that stared out vacantly from behind the grimy windows of the gin parlors, children, women, and old people among them. Poverty and drunkenness went hand in hand. In one of her first dispatches, she described what she had seen:

> Glasgow more resembles an Inferno than any other city we have yet visited. The people are more crowded together, and the stamp of squalid, stolid misery and degradation more obvious and appalling . . . I saw here in Glasgow persons, especially women, dressed in dirty, wretched tatters, worse than none, and with an expression of listless, unexpecting woe upon their faces, far more tragic than the inscription over the gates of Dante's *Inferno*. . . . Glaring throughout Scotland and England is the necessity for the devoutest application of intellect and love to the cure of ills that cry aloud, and, without such application, erelong help *must* be sought by other means than words. . . .
>
> And, though I wish to return to London in the "season" [Margaret and the Springs had arrived there in September, when Parliament was not in session, and most of the wealthy and the aristocracy were at their country homes] . . . I am glad I did not at first see all that pomp and parade of wealth and luxury, in contrast with the misery—squalid, agonizing, ruffianly, which stares one in the face in every street of London, and hoots at the gates of the palaces more ominous a note than ever was that of owl or raven in the portentous times when empires and races have crumbled and fallen from inward decay. . . . Poverty in England has terrors of which I never dreamed at home.

Britain was not the only country with problems. Upheaval and unrest were everywhere. In 1846, only a few months before she left for Europe, Margaret's own country had declared war against Mexico—presumably in response to a series of border conflicts with Texas, which had just been admitted to the Union, but actually, many people believed, in order to extend American territory south and west into Mexican lands, and thereby to extend the slave territories. Margaret hated that war, as did her friends. Emerson denounced it publicly and his protégé and Margaret's old acquaintance Henry Thoreau went even further. As a protest against the war, he refused to pay his poll tax, an act of civil disobedience that cost him a night in jail. There was opposition to the war even in the Congress, and a young first-term congressman from Illinois, Abraham Lincoln, laid his political future on the line by speaking out against it.

Europe was not at war, but it was in turmoil, especially on the Continent. There, the situation was becoming tenser every day. The Industrial Revolution was proceeding more slowly than in Britain, and its dislocations, although dreadful, were less severe. But after the defeat of Napoleon in 1815, the powers that had been allied against France carved up Europe among themselves, installing absolute monarchs on every throne, and backing them up with the force of arms. The people were poor, illiterate, and oppressed. They had no voice in any of the affairs of state, no representation on any government councils —no control whatever over their lives and their futures. They lived in poverty and in terror: the army and the secret police were everywhere, ready to put down any protest, any popular demand for self-government and bread.

One of the countries that was suffering most severely was Italy, which had been parceled out among the Austrians, the Spaniards, and the Papacy; the few Italian monarchs who occupied provincial thrones were merely figureheads. Opposition to this foreign occupation was strong, and since the 1820s, there had been revolutionary societies in Italy dedicated to the unification of the country under one government and to freedom for the Italian people. In London, Margaret met the leader of one of these groups, Giuseppe Mazzini, who had fled his native land to escape execution, and who was still devoting himself, in exile, to his life's goal—the creation of a unified, republican Italy.

Mazzini, who was about Margaret's age, had been a revolutionary since his youth, and in his early twenties had launched a movement, Young Italy, dedicated to independence for his country. "Neither pope nor king, only God and the people will open the way of the future to us," he had written. It was an echo of the spirit that inspired the American Revolution, and its passion and idealism inevitably called forth a response in Margaret. Of all the people she had met in Europe, she enjoyed him the most. Mazzini was, she wrote to Emerson, "a beauteous and pure music," and she was prepared to help him any way she could. He had organized a free night school for the illiterate Italian immigrant boys who roamed London's streets in the hundreds, and one of Margaret's last acts before leaving the city was to visit there and speak to his students.

One piece of unfinished business confronted Margaret during her weeks in London. She had to pay a visit to Mr. Delf, the friend of James Nathan who had been forwarding her letters to him. She had a message to deliver to Nathan through Delf—a message she had been carrying with her since the beginning of September, when she and the Springs were in Edinburgh. She had written to Nathan from there, to plan their meeting in London. But her letter crossed one from him, and his letter made it clear that the meeting would never take place. She should have expected the news it brought; his long silences should have warned her. He was getting married.

"I care not," she wrote in her journal. But, of course, she did. In the last years, since she had left Boston, she had indeed become a public person, who was known everywhere she went. But this recognition was still new. She had felt unlovable for too much of her life to be impervious to any suggestion that she was unlovable still. Nathan's letter was a blow. But she would not let anyone know that. The message she delivered to Delf was short and dignified. "She bade me say to you," he wrote to Nathan, "that she had received your letter, but was too much involved in the routine of visiting and receiving visitors to allow her mind a moment's repose to reply to it."

12

From Paris to Rome

Paris was the next stop after London; Margaret and the Springs were scheduled to stay there nearly three months. It was a less happy time for her than her time in England. First of all, there was the problem of language. Margaret's reading knowledge of French was excellent, but she did not speak it well, and the lessons she began taking as soon as she arrived were not as successful as she would have liked. "My French teacher," she reported to Emerson, "says I speak and act like an Italian." Moreover, France's literary lights were more aloof than Britain's, and Margaret knew no one who could open doors for her. So, although her name was well known in Parisian intellectual circles, she found it difficult to meet people, and she had many fewer social engagements than she had in London. Instead, she did all the proper things for a tourist. She went to the theater and the opera; she visited the museums and the cathedrals; she attended a session of the Chamber of Deputies and a reception at the royal court. And she reported dutifully on all of them for the *Tribune*.

Much that she saw, she did not like. Misery did not clog the streets of Paris as it did in Britain, but it was there, and Margaret sensed it beneath the glitter. On Christmas Eve, she went to Mass at one of the great cathedrals, and was overcome by the irony of the scene. "As I looked on the countenance of the crowd," she wrote, "and saw inscribed there the woes and degradation of which I see such glaring evidence on every side, when I saw the gilt coaches of royalty leaving the door, I marvelled at the faith of men, that they would still be celebrating a fact which at the end of 1800 years has produced so little of the result desired by Jesus."

Still, Paris had its deep rewards. She was given the chance to examine Jean-Jacques Rousseau's manuscripts, which were kept in the library of the Chamber of Deputies. The papers were yellow with the years, and fragile, but they seemed to her alive, and she felt a kind of shiver as she touched them. Rousseau's view of government as a social contract between the people and the state had helped inspire the American Revolution; his belief in man's natural goodness and in the worth of the individual had helped to spark the Transcendentalist revolt. "He was the precursor of all we most prize," she wrote to the *Tribune.* ". . . his spirit was intimate with the fundamental truths of human nature, and fraught with prophecy."

And there was her visit with George Sand, a woman whose life was, to the conventional, even more scandalous and shocking than her novels, with their espousal of socialist causes and their frank depiction of sexual feelings. They could understand Sand's adoption of a masculine pen name—her work might not otherwise have been given serious attention. But they could neither understand nor tolerate the way she lived. She wore men's clothing in public, and publicly smoked cigarettes. And worse: she was separated from her husband, the Baron Dudevant, and had moved from their country estate to Paris, where she lived openly with a series of lovers—with the novelist Jules Sandeau; with the opium-addicted poet Alfred de Musset; with the writer Prosper Mérimée; with the French political philosopher Félicité de Lamennais; when Margaret met her she had been living for twelve years with Frédéric Chopin.

Margaret had always admired Sand's talent and her character, and she had already offended large numbers of readers by mentioning her, without condemnation, in *Woman in the Nineteenth Century* and in one of her articles for the *Tribune.* But she did not offer them a description of her meeting with Mme. Sand. It was somehow too close, too intimate for an article that thousands of the merely curious might read. For Sand was to Margaret courage embodied. She lived her life in accordance with her nature, refusing to be held back by public opinion. To have that courage had always been Margaret's deepest desire for herself. She knew that she and Sand were different in many ways—not only in their backgrounds, but in their characters. Nothing Margaret had ever done in her personal life had been as extravagant or as defiant as the Frenchwoman's conduct. Margaret's rebellions and heresies were not physical, but intellectual. But in many ways, she identified herself with Sand, and the description she wrote of her in a letter to an old Concord friend was one she would have been happy to see written of herself.

> I went to see her at her house, Place d'Orléans. The servant who admitted me . . . announced me as "Madame Salere," and returned into the ante-room to tell me, "Madame says she does not know you." I began to think I was doomed to a rebuff, among the crowd who deserve it. However, to make assurance sure, I said, "Ask if she has not received a letter from me." As I spoke, Madame S. opened the door, and stood looking at me an instant. Our eyes met. I shall never forget her look at that moment. The doorway made a frame for her figure; she is large, but well formed. She was dressed in a robe of dark violet silk, with a black mantle on her shoulders, her beautiful hair dressed with the greatest taste, her whole appearance and attitude, in its simple and lady-like dignity, presenting an almost ludicrous contrast to the vulgar caricature idea of George Sand. . . . What fixed my attention was the expression of good-

ness, nobleness, and power that pervaded the whole—the truly human heart and nature that shone in her eyes. As our eyes met, she said, "*C'est vous*," and held out her hand. I took it, and went into her little study; we sat down a moment, then I said, "*Il me fait de bien de vous voir*," and I am sure I said it with my whole heart, for it made me very happy to see such a woman, so large and so developed a character, and everything that *is* good in it so *really* good. I loved, shall always love her. . . .

She needs no defence, but only to be understood, for she has bravely acted out her nature, and always with good intentions. She might have loved one man permanently, if she could have found one contemporary with her who could interest and command her throughout her range; but there was hardly a possibility of that, for such a person. Thus she has naturally changed the objects of her affection, and several times. Also, there may have been something of the Bacchante in her life, and of the love of night and storm, and the free raptures amid which roamed on the mountain tops the followers of Cybele, the great goddess, the great mother. But she was never coarse, never gross, and I am sure her generous heart has not failed to draw some rich drops from every kind of wine-press. . . .

For the rest, she holds her place in the literary and social world of France like a man, and seems full of energy and courage in it. I suppose she has suffered much, but she has also enjoyed and done much, and her expression is one of calmness and happiness.

At the end of February, Margaret and the Springs left Paris, and a few weeks later they were in Naples, after two boat trips that revived in Margaret all the terror she had felt on the transatlantic crossing. The first was the trip from Marseilles to Genoa. It normally took sixteen hours, but winds and choppy waters nearly doubled the time, and for thirty hours Margaret was sick and terrified. And the trip from Pisa to Naples was even more frightening. Their boat ran headlong into another, coming from the opposite direction. The passengers could see the accident impending. They stood there on the deck, transfixed, watching the inevitable calamity and helpless to do anything. Fortunately, no one was hurt, but everyone was badly frightened.

But no misadventure could permanently spoil Italy for Margaret. She had loved the country and dreamed about it ever since she was a small child struggling to master Latin grammar. She had grown up on tales of the Roman Empire and the Roman Republic; she had felt as close to Romulus and Remus, to Julius Caesar and Marc Antony as to her own brothers. To come to Italy was to come home—to feel a sense of belonging she had never before felt anywhere. In France, she had been a tourist; in England, a visitor. Even in her own country—in Boston, in the West, in New York—there had been that sense of distance and of difference, that indefinable discontent, that almost homesickness.

She still felt it for the first week after her arrival, when she and the Springs were in Genoa. There were still the raw and piercing winds that had slowed their boat and made the trip so unpleasant and, even on land, they threw their chill over everything. "The weather," she wrote to the *Tribune*, "was still so cold I could not realize that I had actually touched those shores to which I had looked forward all my life, where it seemed that the heart would expand and the whole nature be turned to delight. Seen by a cutting wind, the marble palaces, the gardens, the magnificent water-view of Genoa failed to charm—'I *saw*, not *felt*, how beautiful they were.' "

But when they got to Naples, and the winds subsided, she knew she had arrived. ". . . here at Naples, I *have* at last found *my* Italy; I have passed through the Grotto of Pausilippo, visited Cuma, Baiae and Capri, ascended Vesuvius, and found all familiar. . . ." And she was as taken by the Italians as she was by their country. ". . . charming women, refined men, eloquent and courteous."

By April, she and the Springs were in Rome, the place in all of Italy that most profoundly spoke to Margaret's heart. This was the center from which the whole rich culture had radiated. The glories of the ancient city lay in ruins, but newer glories had been erected: the Vatican, St. Peter's Church, the Sistine Chapel. And the ruins still held a spell. "I have heard owls hoot in the Colosseum by moonlight," Margaret wrote; it was wondrous to her. But she was beginning to feel a kind of resentment against the Grand Tour, with its constant travel and sight-seeing. Italy was to her, after all, "my Italy." One lived in one's country; one did not inspect it, as if it were a bolt of cloth, or gaze at its wonders.

"There is very little I can like to write about Italy," she said in a dispatch shortly after she had arrived in Rome. "Italy is beautiful, worthy to be loved and embraced, not talked about . . . It is quite out of the question to know Italy; to say anything of her that is full and sweet, so as to convey any idea of her spirit, without long residence, and residence in the districts untouched by the scorch and dust of foreign invasion (the invasion of the dilettanti, I mean) and without an intimacy of feeling, an abandonment to the spirit of the place. . . ."

And although she and the Springs planned to stay in Rome for two months, that still did not seem to her enough time. There was a special sense of excitement in the city—the feeling that reform and freedom were on their way. Rome was the capital of the Papal States, which for years had suffered under the rule of an autocratic pope, Gregory XVI. But Gregory was now dead and only a few months before Margaret's arrival, a new pope had been elected, Pius IX, who appeared to be far more liberal than his predecessor. Immediately after his installation, he undid some of Gregory's most oppressive acts, granting freedom to nearly four hundred political prisoners, permitting six hundred political exiles to return to Italy, and lightening the heavy press censorship. And shortly after Margaret's arrival in Rome, he issued an edict permitting for the first time the formation of a representative council, whose members would include laymen as well as clergy. The council had no real political power but it did, at least, have the right to make recommendations to him.

To Rome's citizens, all these acts seemed great victories—portents of a peaceful march to democracy. Margaret hoped devoutly that they were right, and she wanted to be in the city to see what would happen, and to give her support to Roman freedom. For the cause of Italy had now become her cause: her talks with Mazzini in London had inspired her. She had to write all the proper travel notes for the *Tribune*, to satisfy her readers, but sight-seeing no longer had anything to do with her real life. Not long after she and the Springs arrived in Rome, she described her feelings in a letter to William Henry Channing:

> I write not to you about these countries, of the famous people I see, of magnificent shows and places. All these things are only to me an illuminated margin on the text of my inward life. Earlier, they would have been more. Art is not important to me now. I like only what little I find that is transcendently good, and even with that feel very familiar and calm. I take interest in the state of the people, their manners, the state of the race in them. I see the future dawning; it is in important aspects Fourier's future. . . .

She was becoming a socialist, a revolutionary—and a Roman. She left the city in June, with the Springs, and traveled with them to Florence, Bologna, and Venice. But there she left them. The Grand Tour had become repugnant to her. It simply made no sense. More than anything else in the world, she wanted to return to Rome. "I should always suffer the pains of Tantalus thinking of Rome," she wrote to her brother Richard from Venice, "if I could not see it more thoroughly than I have yet begun to." She had saved a little money from her earnings, and she was being paid for the articles she wrote for Greeley. It seemed to her she could safely manage in Italy on her own until the next March. Since Rome was deserted during the late summer, she would travel until October at her own pace, in Italy and even for a bit in Switzerland. It might be difficult for a woman to travel alone. But she would do it—and then she would return to Rome.

13
The Cause: Freedom

Despite her commitment to the cause of Italian freedom and her lifelong love affair with Rome, Margaret might not have returned to the city if she had not already made a friend there, someone who knew the city well and could introduce her to its real life. He was Giovanni Angelo Ossoli, a young Roman whom she had known since April.

Their meeting was accidental. During Easter week, she and the Springs had gone to hear Vespers at St. Peter's Church. After the service, they had separated, each to wander at will among the chapels and then to meet, to go back to their rooms. But when Margaret arrived at the spot they had decided on, the Springs were nowhere to be seen. Nor could she find them when she searched in the vastness of the church among the chapels—walking hurriedly, for it was growing dark, stretching her long neck and squinting her nearsighted eyes. And, by these gestures, it was evident to Ossoli, who had also come to Vespers, that she was in distress.

He offered her his help; she accepted, and for a while longer they walked through the silent cavernous church, searching for the Springs. They were, however, no more successful together than Margaret had been alone, and she finally decided to take a carriage back to their lodgings, and meet them there. But there was not a carriage to be found in the piazza in front of the church, and Ossoli volunteered to walk her home.

Their conversation was halting. Margaret's Italian was not yet fluent, and Ossoli knew no English. But she managed to find out some things about him. He was the youngest son of an aristocratic family; like his father, with whom he lived in the family palazzo, he was a *marchese*. For over 150 years, the Ossolis had been connected with the Papacy. His father and his oldest brother were papal functionaries, and his other brothers were colonels in the Pope's Guardia Nobile. But he had no intention of following in any of their footsteps. He was a devout Catholic, and though he believed implicitly in the spiritual leadership of the Pope, he did not believe that the Pope should have temporal power. Nor did he believe in the monarchy. He was a republican, and he looked forward to the day when Italy would be united under a republican government.

It was more than Margaret could have hoped for—to discover, so early in her stay in Rome, a supporter of the cause Mazzini had brought alive for her, and she must have looked at Ossoli with considerable interest. He was, as she could see, quite a bit younger than she was—ten years, as it turned out. And he had the look of a true Roman—dark hair and eyes, a prominent, high-bridged nose, a soft mustache. His voice was gentle, his manner courtly and deferential. His gentleness and his rebellion against the authoritarianism of his papist family reminded her of her brother Eugene, the next oldest to her in the family and her favorite, who had run away from her father's tyranny when the family was living in Groton. She could not help but like him. The Springs, when they met Ossoli, liked him, too, and for the remainder of their visit, he was with them often, showing them Rome as only a Roman could.

When she returned to the city in October, he was even more frequently present, visiting her at her rooms on the Corso, taking her on expeditions to the countryside, introducing her to the cafés where artists and political activists gathered. And he was always solicitous of her, with the special gentleness and courtliness that were among his most endearing qualities. Margaret knew that they were an unlikely couple. Not only because he was so much younger, a Catholic, and an aristocrat, but also because their characters were as unlike as the worlds from which they had come. He was shy and quiet—almost taciturn. She was in love with talk. He had only a conventional Catholic education. He knew art, architecture, and music—they were in the very air he breathed; one could hardly be an aristocrat and not have a sense for them. But he knew almost nothing of the world of books and ideas, and that world was as real to Margaret as any painting or monument.

Yet for all their differences, they shared one important interest and commitment—freedom for Italy. Margaret was thinking of writing a book about the current situation in Rome, and Ossoli, who knew people in all the different political factions—from the papists through the liberals to the radical republicans—was enormously helpful to her. They grew closer and closer.

Margaret was happier than she had ever been before. "Such joy came over me when I was able at last to see Rome again!" she wrote to her mother shortly after her arrival. "To live here alone and independent, to really draw in the spirit of Rome, oh what joy! I know so well how to prize it that I think Heaven will not allow anything to disturb me." And to her brother Richard she wrote at about the same time: "I am now truly happy here, quiet and familiar, no longer a staring, sight-seeing stranger."

Her happiness continued. Once she was settled into her apartment, she began to entertain. Every Monday evening, she was at home to her friends. There was a small American colony in Rome—most of them artists of one sort or another—and they, like Ossoli, were regular visitors. Her friend Christopher Cranch had given up poetry for painting and had come to Italy to study; he and his wife were frequent visitors, as were William Wetmore Story and Emelyn Story, a young Boston couple about Ossoli's age. Story, who was the son of Supreme Court Justice Joseph Story, had attended some of Margaret's Conversations; at the time, he had just been graduated from law school, and was beginning the practice of law. But it had not taken him very long to discover that the law was not his calling, and he was now a sculptor. Emelyn, who had been afraid of Margaret when they first met in Boston, and who had thought of her as "a person on intellectual stilts," became extremely fond of her now that she knew her better, and was quick to sense that her relationship with the young *marchese* was deeper than mere friendship. "There was nothing he would not do for her," Emelyn wrote. "No service was too trivial, no sacrifice too great for him . . . Such tender, unselfish love I have rarely before seen." Margaret's letters home continued to announce her happiness—although they never mentioned Ossoli. "My life in Rome is thus far all I hoped," she wrote her mother in the middle of December. "I have not been so well since I was a child, nor so happy ever, as during the last six weeks." And her dispatch to the *Tribune* positively glowed.

> This 17th day of December I rise to see the floods of sunlight blessing us, as they have almost every day since I returned to Rome—two months and more—with scarce three or four days of rainy weather. I still see the fresh roses and grapes each morning on my table. . . .
>
> How delightful is the contrast between this time and the spring. . . . Then I was here, like travelers in general, expecting to be driven away in a short time. . . .
>
> I now really live in Rome, and I begin to see

> and feel the real Rome. She reveals herself day by day; she tells me something of her life. Now I never go out to see a sight, but I walk every day; here I cannot miss of some object of consummate interest to end a walk.

Then, no more than a few days later, her world smashed into fragments around her. She was, she discovered, pregnant. She was carrying Ossoli's child. In every sense it was a terrible discovery. She was nearly thirty-eight years old—hardly a safe age to give birth for the first time. She had a long history of illness and pain, and was desperately afraid that neither she nor her baby would survive. Even if by some miracle both of them lived, her fright made it impossible for her to see anything but a bleak future for her child.

And then, of course, there were practical problems. She loved Ossoli, and he loved her, but she had never for a moment thought seriously about marrying him. She was content with their relationship as it was. She had struggled all her life for freedom, independence, the chance to live her life on her own terms. Now, she had finally realized her dream. She had seen Britain and France and much of Italy. She was living in her beloved Rome, where great events were in progress. And she was living as she chose—the mistress of her own life. She did not want to trade in her freedom for the "partnership of daily life," as she called it.

Nor, in fact, was marriage all that real a possibility. It would put a financial burden on her that she could not possibly bear. Ossoli, who had no skills and no profession—no way of making a living—was completely dependent on his family. And neither his father nor his older brothers would have countenanced a marriage to Margaret. From every point of view, they would have found her unacceptable. Her age, her nationality, her religion—all of these were shocking enough. But even if they could have brought themselves to come to terms with someone as unlike them as Margaret, even if she had converted to Catholicism or the Pope had granted a dispensation permitting Ossoli to marry her, they could never have accepted her political beliefs. An antipapist, a republican, a follower of Mazzini—such a woman was beyond the pale. If Giovanni married her, they would undoubtedly have cut him off without a cent. He had already offended them sufficiently by joining the Civic Guard—a militia of Roman citizens whose formation the Papal States had been forced, by popular pressure, to authorize.

It seemed to Margaret she had no choice but to keep her pregnancy secret, both from her friends in Rome and her family and friends at home, and to deal with the fact of the baby when—and if—it was safely born. Unlike George Sand, Margaret could not flaunt her rebellions. She would not let the world's opinion prevent her from following her own nature: she had never done it before, and she was not going to begin now. But she would not ask other people to pay, in hurt and worry, for her defiances. And if she made her pregnancy public, her family and friends would pay for it in the ugly comments to which they would be subjected.

Margaret's letters reflected her misery. To Emerson she wrote:

> Nothing less than two or three years, free from care and forced labor would heal all my hurts and renew my life-blood at its source. Since Destiny will not grant me that, I hope she will not leave me long in the world, for I am tired of keeping myself up in the water without corks, and without strength to swim. I should like to go to sleep, and be born again into a state where my young life should not be prematurely taxed. . . .

And to Caroline Sturgis, shortly after the beginning of the year, she said:

> When I arrived in Rome I was at first intoxicated to be here. The weather was beautiful, and many circumstances combined to place me in a kind of passive, child-like well-being. That is all over now, and with this year I enter upon a sphere of my destiny so difficult that I at present see no way out, except through the gate of death. It is useless to write of it; you are at a distance and cannot help me—whether accident or angel will, I have no intimation. I have no reason to hope that I shall not reap what I have sown, and do not. Yet how I shall endure it I cannot guess; it is all a dark, sad enigma.

But however sick and miserable she felt, she must continue to work. The four hundred dollars she had when she arrived in Rome was enough to enable her to live there, frugally, for five or six months. But now she would be remaining considerably longer—at least through the fall. She needed every penny she could earn. Her dispatches to the *Tribune* were her only source of income. She must write them regularly.

And there was ample to write about. England was struggling toward reform—toward giving ordinary people more representation in Parliament and improving the conditions under which they lived and worked. But the tyranny and poverty that Margaret had seen and been shocked by in Paris were still in the saddle throughout the Continent. Everywhere, popular discontent was growing. The people had lived too long with not enough to eat, with backbreaking labor, with rulers who thought of them as draft animals, whose only use was to serve the nobility. If the governments did not voluntarily institute at least some reforms, it could have been predicted that the people would take matters into their own hands.

But instead of reforms, the governments offered repression and provocation: monarchs and noblemen could not be expected to bargain with draft animals. Nor could the Pope, the Prince of the Church in whom at first the Romans had placed such trust: when a delegation of citizens went to the Vatican on New Year's Day to request that he appear in public to bestow his blessings on his subjects, they were curtly refused. "He is tired of these things," a papal official told them; "he is afraid of disturbance." And the monarchies showed their citizens the same contempt. In January, there were uprisings in Genoa, Milan, and Livorno; Sicily, Margaret wrote, "is in full insurrection," and there were reports of revolt in Naples, too.

By February, Ferdinand II of Sicily and the Grand Duke Leopold of Tuscany had been forced to liberalize their constitutions. And France was going up in flames. On the twenty-second of the month, barricades were erected in the streets of Paris; two days later, King Louis-Philippe was forced to abdicate and the Second Republic was proclaimed. March brought the fall of the architect of the whole policy of division and repression: Prince Clemens von Metternich, Austria's minister of foreign affairs, was driven into exile and there were revolutions in Austria, Germany, and Hungary. And in Italy, the revolution continued. On the eighteenth of the month, the Milanese revolted against their Austrian rulers; on the twenty-second, the people of Venice declared their independence from Austria and proclaimed a republic, and on that same day the Piedmontese joined their Venetian and Milanese brothers in war against the Austrians. In Piedmont, King Charles Albert was forced to grant some reforms. So was the Pope.

Margaret reported all these events to her readers back home, in long dispatches full of hope. But by April, she was less optimistic. She could see that freedom would not be achieved easily, and that it would take much time and much struggle to consolidate the achievements of March. In the north, the republican armies were struggling against forces far better equipped than they. And although the Pope had at first supported the moves for freedom, he had finally rejected the revolution and the very idea of Italian independence and unification. On April 19, Margaret reported a speech he had made:

> The Pope declared that he had never any thought of the great results which had followed his actions; that he had only intended local reforms, such as had previously been suggested by the potentates of Europe; that he regretted the *mis*use which had been made of his name; and wound up by lamenting over the war—dear to every Italian heart as the best and holiest cause in which for ages they had been called to embark their hopes—as if it was something offensive to the spirit of religion, and which he would fain see hushed up, and its motives smoothed out and ironed over. . . .
>
> In Rome there is now no anchor except the good sense of the people. . . . All lies in the future; and our best hope must be that the Power which has begun so great a work will find due means to end it, and make the year 1850 a year of true jubilee to Italy; a year not merely of pomps and tributes, but of recognized rights and intelligent joys; a year of real peace—peace founded not on compromise and the lying etiquettes of diplomacy, but on truth and justice. . . .
>
> My friends write to urge my return; they talk of our country as the land of the future. It is so, but that spirit which made it all it is of value in my eyes, which gave all of hope with which I can sympathize for that future, is more

> alive here at present than in America. My country is at present spoiled by prosperity, stupid with the lust of gain, soiled by crime in its willing perpetuation of slavery. . . . In Europe amid the teachings of adversity a nobler spirit is struggling—a spirit which cheers and animates mine. I hear earnest words of pure faith and love. I see deeds of brotherhood. This is what makes *my* America. I do not deeply distrust my country. She is not dead but in my time she sleepeth, and the spirit of our fathers flames no more, but lies hid beneath the ashes. . . . Here things are before my eyes worth recording, and if I cannot help this work, I would gladly be its historian.

On May 13, Margaret wrote a postscript to this dispatch. Rome was restive. Its citizens still wanted to trust their Pope, but the movement for reform was at a standstill, and little had been achieved. But the city was still beautiful. "The nightingales sing," Margaret wrote; "every tree and plant is in flower, and the sun and moon shine as if paradise were already established on earth. I go to one of the villas to dream it is so beneath the pale light of the stars."

The villa that she referred to was in Aquila, a quiet, remote village in the Apennines. On May 24, Margaret left Rome. It was time for her departure. If she had remained in the city much longer, her pregnancy would have become evident to everyone.

14

Viva la Republica! Viva Italia!

Aquila was a charming village, its ruined temples and amphitheaters rich with reminders of Rome's great days. But the months Margaret spent there were full of fear and unhappiness. She was alone, except for a maid. Ossoli's commitment to the Civic Guard made it impossible for him to leave Rome except occasionally, and then only for very short periods. He visited her as often as he could, and wrote her—as she wrote him—several times each week, enclosing with his letters newspapers and other journals he knew would interest her. But that was hardly enough. Margaret felt isolated from everything that mattered to her. She had no one to talk to; she was miles away from the daily events of the revolution; she had no work to do: the *Tribune* was not interested in articles about life in a remote

Italian mountain town, no matter how romantic the setting or how exotic the townspeople. She felt as if her whole world had melted, leaving her unprotected and alone.

Added to all of this were the difficulties of her pregnancy. She was ill a great deal of the time, and her pain only increased her fear and loneliness. She tried to still her misery by throwing herself into an orgy of letter writing—to more than a hundred people. One of them was Caroline Sturgis—now Caroline Sturgis Tappan. By the time Margaret got to Aquila, her finances had been almost depleted, and among her other problems was the problem of money. So she turned to Caroline, who had been a friend for so long, to ask for a small loan. Out of her need to justify the request—which, to her Puritan conscience was almost sinful—and her need to open her heart to a friend, she finally described her situation and her fears for herself and the child she was about to bear. Caroline responded as Margaret hoped she would, with support and love and with the offer to take the baby and raise it as her own, should anything happen to Margaret or Ossoli. But even Caroline's warmth and friendship could not quiet Margaret's fears. The only relief she felt was when she saw Ossoli. So at the end of July she moved to Rieti, a somewhat larger town, closer to Rome, where Ossoli would be able to visit her more often.

By the middle of August, the wait for the baby's arrival and her fears for her own life had become almost intolerable. "If I were sure of doing well," she wrote Ossoli on August 22, "I should wish to pass through this trial before your arrival, but when I think it is possible for me to die alone, without the touch of one dear hand, I wish to wait no longer. So I hope for your presence on Sunday morning."

He did not come that Sunday, but he was there the next. "Tomorrow I leave Rome," he had written her, "and I hope to have you in my arms Sunday." And when he arrived, he could see what Margaret knew already—that the baby was coming at last. Her pains had started, and they were severe. She labored for two full days—Sunday and Monday. Finally, on Tuesday, September 5, their son was born.

His birth was a miracle to Margaret, and her feelings for him surprised her in their intensity. She had loved Emerson's son, Waldo; and the Greeleys' little boy, Pickie; she loved Eddie Spring. But her feelings for them, she discovered, were nothing as compared with her feelings for her own child. He was all her life. She panicked when, only a few days after his birth, she developed a fever and had to stop nursing him. She panicked again when the child of the wet nurse became ill: the woman might not now be able to nurse her baby. And even when the nurse's child recovered, she was still in fear. She wrote Ossoli, who had returned to Rome:

> One must have courage, but it is a great care to be staying alone and ignorant with a baby in the first days of its life. When he is a month old, I will feel more relaxed. . . . He is beginning to sleep well, and he is very handsome for his age. Everyone around here, without knowing what name I thought of giving him, calls him Angio-

> lino [little angel] because he is so pretty. He has your mouth, hands and feet. I think his eyes will be blue. For the rest, he is altogether an imp. He understands well, and is very obstinate about having his own way. . . .

The baby survived the first month, and Margaret's anxieties abated somewhat. But now she and Ossoli were confronted with difficult practical problems. They had no intention, yet, of making the baby's birth public. Margaret could hardly announce herself as the mother of a child without at the same time announcing its father. Nor could she announce the child's father, except as her husband. It would have been too shocking; it would have broken her mother's heart. And she and Ossoli could not marry. It would have cost him all his connections with his family—not only financial, but personal, as well. The family was the mooring of every Italian's life. To cut oneself adrift from it was simply unthinkable.

But Margaret could not remain in Rieti forever. Nor could she bring the baby back with her to Rome. For a while, she fantasized about finding a wet nurse in the city, with whom to board her child. But, attractive as the dream was, she knew it was impossible. If the baby was in Rome, people would learn of it, sooner or later. So she began a search to find someone reliable to leave her infant with in Rieti.

Meanwhile, Ossoli was wrestling with another problem. The baby needed a certificate of baptism—not only because his father was a devout Catholic, and baptism was important to him, but for practical reasons, too. In the Papal States, where church and government were one, a certificate of baptism was, in effect, a birth certificate. Without it, the baby would have no legal existence and no legal rights. But the document required the names of the child's parents, and that would leak the secret. Frantically, Ossoli searched around for a way to have the baby baptized without revealing his mother's name. It took more than a month of legal maneuvering—and probably some bribery. While he was struggling with the negotiations, a near calamity arose. There was an outbreak of smallpox in Rieti, and the local doctor had already used up his supply of vaccine by the time he arrived at Margaret's lodgings—days after she had first asked him to come. Near hysteria, she wrote Ossoli. Somehow, somewhere, he must get his hands on vaccine for their son. He managed to, and sent the package to her.

And he managed, too, to complete arrangements to have the baby baptized in such a way that his mother's name would not be revealed and, at the same time, his rights to his Ossoli inheritance would be protected. On November 6, 1848, when he was two months and one day old, Angelo Eugenio Filippo Ossoli was baptized in a small church in Rieti. And shortly thereafter, his tearful mother left him in the care of a wet nurse—a cheerful young peasant woman named Chiara—and returned to Rome.

During the time Margaret was in the mountains, the struggle for Italian unification and freedom had suffered desperate blows. In Naples, the revolution had been crushed by Swiss mercenaries; in the Piedmont area, by the armies of Austria; and in Rome, the Pope had appointed a prime minister, Pellegrino Rossi, whom the people detested. Under his leadership, some of the worst of the old repressions had been reinstituted. His political opponents were arrested and sent into exile; the press and the mail were once again censored; and troops had been sent to put down popular uprisings in the outlying parts of the Papal States. By the time Margaret arrived in Rome, popular anger was high, and the Pope—in whom his subjects had once placed such confidence—had become no more than a figurehead, frightened and isolated in the Papal Palace. She had been there no more than a few days when Rome's great drama began to unfold.

It started on November 15, when Rossi was assassinated—stabbed to death in the courtyard of the Chancellory. Margaret wrote in the *Tribune*,

> His carriage approached, attended by a howling, hissing multitude. He smiled, affected unconcern, but must have felt relieved when his horses entered the courtyard gate of the *Cancelleria*. He did not know he was entering the place of his execution. The horses stopped, he alighted in the midst of a crowd; it jostled him as if for the purpose of insult; he turned abruptly, and received as he did so the fatal blow. It was dealt by a resolute, perhaps experienced hand; he fell and spoke no word more.
>
> The crowd, as if all previously acquainted with the plan, as no doubt most of them were, issued quietly from the gate and passed through

> the outside crowd—its members, among whom was he who dealt the blow, dispersing in all directions. . . .

The drama heightened the next day, when the Pope's Swiss Guard opened fire on a crowd of Romans who had gone to the Papal Palace to demand reforms. Margaret wrote to her mother,

> Today all the troops and the people united and went to the Quirinal to demand a change of measures. They found the Swiss Guard drawn out, and the Pope dared not show himself. They attempted to force the door of his palace, to enter his presence, and the guard fired. I saw one man borne by, wounded. . . .
>
> Late at night the Pope had to yield, but not till the door of his palace was half burst, and his confessor killed. This man, Parma, provoked his fate by firing on the people from a window. It seems the Pope never gave the order to fire; his Guard acted from a sudden impulse of their own. The new ministry chosen are little inclined to accept. It is almost impossible for anyone to act, unless the Pope is stripped of his temporal power, and the hour for that is not yet quite ripe; though they talk more and more of proclaiming the Republic, and even of calling my friend Mazzini. . . .

By now the Pope was in panic. He could not form a new government, and he dared not take the reins into his own hands. It seemed to him that he was a prisoner. On November 24, less than two weeks after Rossi's assassination, he fled from Rome; in the dead of night and in disguise, he rode out of the city in a borrowed coach, traveling north along the Appian Way to the fortress of Gaeta, where he would be under the protection of the restored Neapolitan monarchy.

Margaret could not help but sympathize with his sense of helplessness. But she was a republican, and the daughter of a revolution which had been fought to establish religious freedom and to separate church and state. She wrote in the *Tribune*,

> Poor Pope, how has his mind been torn to pieces in these later days. It moves compassion. There can be no doubt that all his natural impulses are generous, and kind, and in a more private station he would have died beloved and honored, but to this he was unequal; he has suffered bad men to surround him, and by their misinterpretations and insidious suggestions at last entirely to cloud his mind. . . .
>
> No more of him! His day is over. He has been made, it seems, unconsciously an instrument of good his regrets cannot destroy. . . . These acts have not had the effect the foes of freedom hoped. Rome remained cool and composed; all felt that they had not demanded more than was their duty to demand; and were willing to accept what might follow. In a few days all began to say: "Well, who would have thought it? The Pope, the Cardinals, the Princes are all gone, and Rome is perfectly tranquil and does not miss anything, except that there are not so many rich carriages and liveries. . . ."

That tranquillity gave Margaret time to think about her own problems. They were formidable. Her baby was miles from her. She missed him desperately and worried constantly that he was not getting adequate care. And it was a torture to her not to be able to tell anyone about him. The real Angelino was a beautiful active blue-eyed baby boy, his parents' greatest joy and fulfillment, but the idea of Angelino was a scandal—an outrage against every propriety of Margaret's Puritan world.

Still, she had not been able to resist a hint in the letter she wrote her mother right after her return to Rome.

> Of other circumstances which complicate my position I cannot write. Were you here, I would confide in you fully, and have more than once in the silence of the night recited to you these most strange and romantic chapters in the story of my sad life . . . I am sure you will always love your daughter, and will know gladly in all events she has tried to aid and striven never to injure her fellows. In earlier days I dreamed of doing and being much, but now am content with the Magdalene to rest my plea hereon: "She has loved much."

The more she thought about her situation, the more she realized how unjust it was—how much unhappiness she was asked to accept simply because she was a woman. No one would reject a man for fathering a child out of wedlock, as long as he acknowledged his legal obligation to the child. It was a woman's name, not a man's, that was traditionally used to describe the sinner against society's sexual conventions—the Mary Magdalene with whom Margaret had associated herself in her letter to her mother. Her anger and despair spilled out at the end of her dispatch describing the revolution in Rome:

> Pray send here a good ambassador . . . a man of unity in principles, but capable of understanding variety in forms. And send a man capable of prizing the luxury of living in or knowing Rome; the office of ambassador is one that should not be thrown away on a person who cannot prize or use it. Another century and I might ask to be made ambassador myself . . . but woman's day has not come yet. . . . How much I shall have to say on that subject if I live, which I desire not, for I am very tired of the battle with great wrongs, and would like to have someone younger and stronger arise to say what ought to be said, still more to do what might be done. Enough! If I felt these things in privileged America, the cries of [Roman] mothers and wives beaten at night by sons and husbands for their diversion after drinking . . . have sharpened my perception of the ills of woman's condition and the remedies that must be applied. Had I but genius, had I but energy to tell what I know as it ought to be told! God grant them me, or some other more worthy woman, I pray.

This dispatch was dated December 2; when a few weeks had passed and the city was still tranquil, Margaret permitted herself to feel the full force of her longing to see her baby, and on the morning of December 21, she left Rome for Rieti, to spend Christmas with Angelino and to reassure herself that he was in good hands. The day was bitter cold, and the heavy gray sky portended snow, but she made the long trip safely and by 4:30 that afternoon was holding her child in her arms. He seemed to be healthy. "He sleeps so well at night," she wrote Ossoli, who had been promoted to sergeant in the Civic Guard and had not been able to leave with her, "cries very rarely, and then not hard. . . . When I held him, he leaned his dear head a long time on my shoulder. At night I very much enjoyed sleeping with him. . . ." Still, she worried. The house was cold and drafty; the baby had been sick and the doctor had not come; the wet nurse and her family were kind, but uneducated and unpredictable. She trusted them to care about the baby; she did not trust them always to deal wisely with his needs. But on the whole, her visit was reassuring, and at the end of the month, she was ready to return.

In Rome, the revolution was progressing despite a decree sent by the Pope from Gaeta on January 6 excommunicating everyone associated with the movement to strip him of his temporal power. The Romans found the papal manifesto contemptible. Margaret wrote:

> The procession which carried it, mumbling chants, for deposit in places provided for lowest uses . . . was a real and generous expression of popular disgust. From that hour, the power of

> the scarlet hierarchy fell to rise no more. No authority can survive a universal moment of derision. From that hour, tongues and pens were loosed . . . and people talked as they felt, just as those of us who do not choose to be slaves are accustomed to do in America. . . . All felt that . . . it only remained to organize another form of government.

And that the Roman people did just one month later. On February 8, 1849, the General Assembly opened. For the first time, every Roman man over twenty-one had been allowed to vote for its membership. The assembly met throughout the day and into the evening. Margaret wrote:

> An immense crowd of people surrounded the Palazzo della Cancelleria, within whose courtyard Rossi fell, while the debate was going on within. At one o'clock in the morning of the 9th of February, a republic was resolved upon, and the crowd rushed away to ring all the bells.

The Papacy had fallen; Rome was to be a pure democracy; the dream had been realized.

15
The Siege of Rome

The first days of the Roman Republic were tranquil, and the people behaved with enormous discipline:

> The day after the proclamation of the Republic, some zealous ignoramuses insulted the carriages that appeared with servants in livery. The ministry published a grave admonition that democracy meant liberty, not license, and that he who infringed upon an innocent freedom of action in others must be declared traitor to his country. Every act of the kind ceased instantly. An intimation that it was better not to throw large comfits or oranges during Carnival, as injuries have thus been sometimes caused, was obeyed with equal docility.

But the calm seemed to Margaret deceptive—even ominous. The republic had too many enemies. The Pope in Gaeta and the papists still in the city, the Austrian monarchy and the French Republic of Louis Napoleon all had a stake in the restoration of the Pope to temporal power. For the Pope and his followers, it was the long, unbroken tradition of church control over the government of Rome; for the Austrians, it was fear of the republican movement in the provinces they ruled; for Louis Napoleon, it was the debt he owed to the papists, who had helped put him in power, as well as his fear that the Austrians might become the rulers of Rome. Margaret hoped and prayed that there would be no intervention against the Republic, but she was far from sure.

Her anxieties were somewhat allayed by an act of the assembly only a few days after the Republic was formed. Mazzini was invited to return from his exile and was made a member of the Assembly and a citizen of the Republic. Mazzini arrived in Rome on March 5, and three days later paid an unannounced visit to Margaret, knocking on her door and calling out her name. She recognized his voice immediately. "He looks," she wrote to Marcus Spring, "more divine than ever, after all his new, strange sufferings. . . . If anyone can save Italy from her foes, inward and outward, it will be he. But he is very doubtful whether this be possible; the foes are too many, too strong, too subtle. . . . He looks as if the great battle he has fought had been too much for his strength, and that he was only sustained by the fire of his soul."

He gave her a ticket to the Assembly, and she was present when he made his first speech. His voice was quiet, almost conversational, as he offered his listeners a history of their city, ending in triumphant hope. "After the Rome which wrought by conquest of arms, the Rome which wrought by conquest of words, must come a third which shall work by virtue of example. After the Rome of the emperors, after the Rome of the Popes, will come the Rome of the People. The Rome of the People is arisen . . . let us rejoice together."

The chance for rejoicing meant, for Margaret, the chance to see her son again. For as long as Rome was calm, she felt free to leave. She found Angelino in good health and, to her enormous relief, he seemed to recognize her: for these reasons, her visit was reassuring. But she was frightened of what might happen to him if the political situation worsened and communication was cut off between Rieti and Rome. She was also frightened by the evidence she had already seen, in Rieti, of the ignorance and unreliability of the people there. In a long letter to Caroline, begun before she left for Rieti and finished after she returned, Margaret described her fears and her situation:

> My baby saw mountains when he first looked forward into the world. Rieti, not only an old classic town of Italy, but one founded by what are now called the aborigines, is a hive of very ancient dwellings with soft red-brown roofs, a citadel, and several towers. It is in a plain, twelve miles in diameter one way, not much less

the other, entirely encircled with mountains of the noblest form. . . .

I intend to write all that relates to the birth of Angelino in a little book, which I shall, I hope, show you some time. I have begun it and then stopped; it seemed to me he would die. If he lives, I shall finish it, before the details are at all faded in my mind. Rieti is a place where I should have liked to have him born, and where I should like to have him now, but that the people are so wicked, the most ferocious and mercenary population of Italy. . . . Me they were bent on plundering in every way. . . . They made me suffer terribly in the first days and disturb me greatly still in visits to my darling. . . .

You say no secret can be kept in the civilized world and suppose not long, but it is very important to me to keep this, for the present, if possible, and by and by to have the mode of disclosure at my option. For this I have made the cruellest sacrifices; it will, indeed, be just like the rest, if they are made of none effect.

After I wrote you, I went to Rieti. . . . When I first took my darling little child in my arms he made no sound but leaned his head against my bosom, and stayed so, he seemed to say how could you abandon me. What I felt you will know only when you have your own. A little girl who lived in the house told me all the day of my departure he would not be comforted, always refusing the breast and looking at the door; he has been a strangely precocious infant; I think it was through sympathy with me, and that in that regard it may be a happiness for him to be with these more plebeian, instinctive, joyous

> natures. I saw he was more serene, that he was not sensitive as when with me, and slept a great deal more. You speak of my being happy, all the solid happiness I have ever known has been at times when he went to sleep in my arms . . . I do not look forward to his career and his manly life; it is *now* I want to be with him, before prescience ends and bafflings begin. If I had a little money I should go with him into strict retirement for a year or two and live for him alone. This I cannot do: all life that has been or could be natural to me is invariably denied. God knows why, I suppose.
>
> I receive with profound gratitude your thought of taking him, if anything should happen to us . . . I shall think about it. Before he was born, I did a great deal, having the idea I might die and all my spirit remain incarnated in him, but now I think I shall live and carry him round myself, as I ride on my ass into Egypt.
>
> You talk about your mangers, Carrie, but that was only for a little, presently came kings with gold cups and all sorts of things. Joseph pawned them; with part of the money he bought this nice donkey for the journey; and they lived on the rest till Joseph could work at his trade. We have no donkey and it costs a great deal to travel in diligences and steamers, and being a nobleman is a poor trade in a ruined despotism just turning into a Republic. . . .

All the complaints she had voiced to Caroline about the Rietini, and all her fears of their violence were further aroused during the visit she was now paying her child. A few days after her arrival, she wrote to Ossoli in near panic.

> Yesterday the family was downstairs at supper and our dear one upstairs asleep in bed. I was sitting at his side thinking how sweet because I had washed him and dressed him and he looked like another child. Suddenly I heard, from below, table and chairs falling and women crying terribly for help. I flew downstairs and found Pietro and Nicola trying to kill one another. I spoke to Nicola and he didn't answer, just looked at me like a wild animal. The women were holding his arms so that he couldn't get his knife, and he was pulling their hair. Pietro, who didn't have a knife, threw a big piece of wood, which missed my head by inches. All the neighbors came running immediately, and Nicola's employer seized his knife; but if our child had been downstairs, it is probable that he would have been killed. . . .

The hysteria eventually died down. But the incident did nothing to reassure Margaret about the safety of her child. "I think God sent me to protect him during these terrible days," she wrote Ossoli a few days later. "Nicola was crazy for more than 40 hours, with Chiara desperate, crying continually."

But to bring Angelino back to Rome with her would be an act of madness. No one knew from day to day how safe the city was. The situation had already begun to worsen while Margaret was in Rieti. Inspired by the Republic, the people of Piedmont, in the north, forced their king to take up arms against the occupying Austrians. The Piedmontese fought bravely, but they were outnumbered and outarmed and their troops were routed only a few days after the uprising began.

That defeat spelled the beginning of the end for the Roman Republic. The French, frightened by this demonstration of Austrian strength, sent what they described as a "protective" force to save Rome from Austria, landing twelve thousand soldiers in Civitavecchia, near Rome, in early April. From his garrison in Civitavecchia, the French general Oudinot began a whole series of stratagems and negotiations designed to bring Rome into his hands. He had come, he said, as a "friend and brother," and he requested that Rome open its gates to him and his troops. The request was rejected, and throughout April, while notes continued to pass between the French and the Roman governments, now headed by a triumvirate of which Mazzini was a member, Oudinot's army held Rome in a vise. Margaret returned from her visit to her child to a city whose citizens were locked inside it like animals in a cage, to a city where war was imminent. On April 26, Oudinot sent an agent to Mazzini with what was, in effect, an ultimatum. The French would aid the Republic against the Austrians, if they should march south; in exchange, the republic would restore the Pope as the head of government. Mazzini rejected the proposal. "Rome is barricaded," Margaret wrote in her journal, "and the foe daily, hourly expected. . . . From my window I see now where they are hanging boards. I suppose to make a support for cannon, and it seems to be such play for men and boys alike."

But whatever it seemed to be, it was not play. On April 30, while still protesting their peaceful intentions, the French began their siege of Rome. Ossoli, now a sergeant in the Republican Army, was stationed on the wall defending the Vatican—the wall the French were hourly expected to attack. His position was exposed and dangerous.

But Margaret had little time to frighten herself with thoughts of what might happen to him. On the very morning that Oudinot's troops attacked, a letter was hand-delivered to her by a messenger for the Princess di Belgioioso, an old acquaintance who, like Ossoli, had rejected the traditional papist loyalties of the aristocracy and had allied herself with the Republic.

"Dear Miss Fuller," the note read. "You are named Regolatrice of the Hospital of the Fate Bene Fratelli. Go there at 12 if the alarm bell does not ring before. When you arrive there, you will receive all the women coming for the wounded and give them your directions so that you are sure to have a certain number of them, night and day. May God help us. Cristina Trivulzio di Belgioioso."

Margaret sped to the hospital on the Tiber Island. Months later, she wrote to William Henry Channing of her feelings at that time. Her emotions were wrenched almost beyond endurance by the human cost of the war. And, although she did not say it in the letter, by terror for the people she most loved—

Ossoli, under the constant threat of French cannon, and her baby, miles away, in the care of people she did not trust, in a place the war might reach, a place that was now cut off from any communication with Rome:

> You say you are glad I have had this great opportunity for carrying out my principles. Would it were so! I found myself inferior in courage and fortitude to the occasion. I knew not how to bear the havoc and anguish incident to the struggle for these principles. I rejoice that it lay not with me to cut down the trees, to destroy the Elysian gardens, for the defense of Rome; I do not know that I could have done it. And the sight of these far nobler growths, the beautiful young men, mown down in their stately prime, became too much for me. I forgot the great ideas, to sympathize with the poor mothers, who had nursed their precious forms, only to see them all lopped off and gashed. You say, I sustained them; often have they sustained my courage; one, kissing the pieces of bone that were so painfully extracted from his arm, hanging them round his neck to be worn as the true relics of today; mementoes that he also had done and borne something for his country and the hopes of humanity. One fair young man, who is made a cripple for life, clasped my hands as he saw me crying over the spasms I could not relieve, and faintly cried, "*Viva l'Italia.*" "Think only, *cara bona donna*," said a poor wounded soldier, "that I can always wear my uniform on *festas*, just as it is now, with the holes where the balls

> went through, for a memory." "God is good; God knows," they often said to me, when I had not a word to cheer them.

Margaret was unfair to herself and to the work she was doing. Emelyn Story, who called her a "mild saint and a ministering angel," gave a much truer picture of her during those terrible days:

> I have walked with Margaret through the wards, and seen how comforting was her presence to the poor, suffering men. "How long will the Signora stay? When will the Signora come again?" they eagerly asked. For each one's peculiar tastes she had a care; to one she carried books; to another she told the news of the day; and listened to another's oft-repeated tale of wrongs as the best sympathy she could give. They raised themselves on their elbows to get the last glimpse of her as she was going away.

By now, Margaret had given up her apartment and moved in with the Storys, whose quarters were in a section somewhat safer from enemy fire. Every day, she made her rounds at the hospital; as each group of the wounded was brought in she had to fight her terror that Ossoli might be among them. Every evening that she could, she packed a basket of provisions and set out on the hazardous trip through the city to visit with Ossoli at his post on the walls. He refused to leave it, but remained there constantly, snatching a few hours of sleep whenever he could. Nor would he keep for himself the food she had brought. He shared everything with his comrades.

With all her duties and all her terrors, Margaret still found time to write for the *Tribune*, reporting on the diplomatic maneuvers that still continued within the sound of cannonading; on the bombardments and battles and skirmishes; on the destruction of some of Rome's most beautiful gardens and monuments; on the bravery of the soldiers; on the steadfastness of the Roman people; and on the persistence of the Triumvirate—despite all provocations—in its efforts to find some way, outside of further bloodshed, to enable the Republic to endure.

As the battles and the diplomatic maneuvers continued, Margaret's fears of the outcome mounted. Rome stood alone, one enemy at its walls, others likely to arrive momentarily. It seemed almost impossible that the Republic could survive. Ossoli, at his exposed post, was in constant danger. As for herself, she was so weary and so despairing she did not see how she could live through the next months. But what would happen to Angelino without her and Ossoli? She had to make some provision for him. So far only Caroline knew of his existence. Someone in Rome had to be told. That person, obviously, was Emelyn. And only Emelyn. She must not tell her husband. The story that Margaret reported to her embroidered a trifle on the truth. She said that she and Ossoli were married. And in every sense but the purely legal, they were. Their lives were bound together, by their love and by their child.

Emelyn wrote of Margaret's dilemma at that time,

> I well remember how exhausted and weary she was; how pale and agitated she returned to us after her day's and night's watching; how eagerly she asked for news of Ossoli. . . .
>
> After one such day, she called me to her bedside and said that I must consent, for her sake, to keep the secret she was now about to confide. Then she told me of her marriage; where her child was, and where he was born; and gave me certain papers and parchment documents which I was to keep; and in the event of her and her husband's death I was to take the boy to her mother in America, and confide him to her care and that of her friend Mrs. Caroline Sturgis Tappan. . . .
>
> The papers thus given me, I had perfect liberty to read; but after she had told me her story, I desired no confirmation of this fact, beyond what her words had given. . . . There was also a book, in which Margaret had written the history of her acquaintance and marriage with Ossoli, and of the birth of her child. In giving that to me, she said, "If I do not survive to tell this myself to my family, this book will be to them invaluable. If I live, it will be of no use, for my word will be all that they will ask." I took the papers and locked them up. . . .

It was a relief to Margaret to have confided in Emelyn. She sent a message to Ossoli at his post, telling him that she had. "In the event of the death of both of us, I have left a paper with a certificate in regard to Angelino, and some lines praying the Storys to take care of him. If by any accident *I* die, you can revoke this paper if you will . . . I have wished Nino to go to America, but you will do as seems best to you. We ought to have planned this better . . . If you live and I die, be always most devoted to Nino. If you ever love another, think first of him. I pray, pray, love."

16

The Death of the Republic

All through May and June, the siege of Rome continued. Every day, Margaret was at the hospital, tending the wounded: talking to them, listening to them, trying—despite her misery—to cheer them somehow. Ossoli remained at his station, unflinching in his devotion to the Republic. He had by now been promoted to captain, and his increased responsibilities brought him into greater danger of enemy fire.

At the end of May, the Storys left Rome. They had two children; with the French coming ever closer, they no longer felt it safe to remain. Most of the American colony had long since departed, and now only a few remained. Among them were the painter, Thomas Hicks, who did Margaret's portrait, the portrait of a weary and despairing woman; and the United States chargé d'affaires, Lewis Cass, Jr., whose position in Rome was ambiguous. The modern world's first republic had not yet extended recognition to the Roman Republic. It was a bitter fact for Margaret, and it only added to her sense of hopelessness. In a dispatch to the *Tribune* written at the end of May, she pleaded with her countrymen:

> It seems to me that the only dignified ground for our government, the only legitimate ground for any republican government, is to recognize for any nation the government chosen by itself. The suffrage has been correct here, and the proportion of votes to the whole population was much larger, it was said by Americans here, than it is in our own country at the time of contested elections. It had elected an Assembly; that Assembly had appointed to meet the exigencies of this time the Triumvirate. If any misrepresentations have induced America to believe, as France affects to have believed, that so large a vote could have been obtained by moral intimidation, the present unanimity of the population in resisting such immense odds, and the enthusiasm of their every expression in favor of the present government, put the matter beyond a doubt. The Roman people claims once more to have a national existence. It declines further serfdom to an ecclesiastical court. It claims liberty of conscience, of action, and of thought. Should it fall from its present position, it will not be from internal dissent, but from foreign oppression.
>
> Since this is the case, surely our country, if

> no other, is bound to recognize the present government *so long as it can sustain itself*. . . .
>
> Send, dear America, to thy ambassador a talisman precious beyond all that boasted gold of California. Let it loose his tongue to cry, "Long Live the Republic, and may God bless the cause of the people, the brotherhood of nations and of men—the equality of rights for all." "*Viva America!*"

Cass's dispatches to the State Department were less passionately worded, but they echoed Margaret's hopes. But no word came from the United States. In the eyes of the American government, the Roman Republic did not exist. Still, Rome fought on, against increasingly uneven odds. The negotiations between the Triumvirate and Oudinot continued, fruitlessly. And although the Romans looked forward daily to some word from the French government—a recall of its troops, a reversal of its declared intention to restore the Pope—no such word came. Margaret's dispatches in June reflected the worsening situation:

> What shall I write of Rome in these sad but glorious days? Plain facts are the best, for my feelings I could not find fit words. . . .
>
> Since the 3rd we have only cannonade and skirmishes. The French are at their trenches, but cannot advance much; they are too much molested from the wall. The Romans have made one very successful sortie. The French availed themselves of a violent thunderstorm, when the

> walls were left more thinly guarded, to try to scale them, but were immediately driven back. It was thought by many that they never would be willing to throw bombs and shells into Rome, but they do whenever they can. . . .

And, a few days later:

> Yes, the French, who pretend to be the advanced guard of civilization, are bombarding Rome! They dare take the risk of destroying the richest bequests made to man by the great past! Nay, they seem to do it in an especially barbarous manner. It was thought they would avoid as much as possible the hospitals for the wounded, marked to their view by the black banner, and the places where are the most precious monuments; but several bombs have fallen on the chief hospital, and the Capitol evidently is especially aimed at. They made a breach in the wall, but it was immediately filled up with a barricade, and all week they have been repulsed in every attempt they made to gain ground, though with considerable loss of life on our side; on theirs it must be great, but how great we cannot know.
>
> Ponte Molle, the scene of Raphael's fresco of a battle in the Vatican, saw again a fierce struggle last Friday. More than fifty were brought wounded into Rome.
>
> But wounds and assaults only fire more and more the courage of her defenders. They feel the justice of their cause, and the peculiar iniquity of this aggression. In proportion as there seems little aid to be hoped from man,

they seem to claim it from God. The noblest sentiments are heard from every lip, and thus far their acts amply correspond. . . .

Meanwhile, many poor people are driven from their homes, and provisions are growing very dear. The heats are now terrible for us. . . .

As to the men who die, I share the impassioned sorrow of the Triumvirs. "O Frenchmen!" they wrote. "Could you know what men you destroy! *They* are no mercenaries like those who fill your ranks, but the flower of the Italian youth and the noblest among the aged. When you shall know of what minds you have robbed the world, how ought you to repent and mourn!"

This is especially true of the Emigrant and Garibaldi Legions. The misfortunes of Northern and Southern Italy, the conscription which compels to the service of tyranny those who remain, has driven from the kingdom of Naples and from Lombardy all the brave and noble youth. . . . Many of these young men, students from Pisa, Pavia, Padua, and the Roman University, lie wounded in the hospitals, for naturally they rushed first to the combat. One kissed an arm which was cut off, another preserves pieces of bone which were painfully extracted from his wound as relics of the best days of his life. The older men, many of whom have been saddened by exile and disappointment, less glowing, are not less resolved. A spirit burns noble as ever animated by the most precious deeds we treasure from the heroic age. I suffer to see these temples of the soul thus broken, to see the fever-weary days and painful operations undergone by these noble men, these true priests of a higher hope;

> but I would not for much have missed seeing it all. The memory of it will console amid the spectacles of meanness, selfishness and faithlessness which life may yet have in store for the pilgrim.
>
> In the evening 'tis pretty though terrible to see the bombs, fiery meteors, springing from the horizon line upon their bright path to do their wicked message. 'Twould not be so bad, methinks, to die by one of these as wait to have every drop of pure blood, every childlike radiant hope drained and driven from the heart by the betrayals of nations and of individuals, till at last the sickened eyes refuse more to open to that light which shines daily on such pits of iniquity.

Margaret wrote these words on June 23. From that day, matters for the Republic became steadily worse. The French bombardment increased daily, and daily the French troops advanced closer to the city. The Republic had no help from anywhere. Supplies were dwindling. No more than three or four cannon remained to defend the city. Only a miracle could save it.

On the afternoon of June 30, Margaret sent a note to Lewis Cass, asking him if he would call on her. He hurried over, and found her lying, pale and trembling, on a sofa, exhaustion written in every line of her face. She told him, as she had told Emelyn Story, that she was married to Ossoli, and that she did not believe he or his troops could survive the bombardment the French would surely level against their station on the Pincian Hill that night. She was going, she told him, to join her husband at his post. She did not expect either of them to return. She gave Cass some papers and asked him, if she did not come back, to send them to friends in America.

As the bells were ringing out the Ave Maria, Ossoli came for her. Together they set out across the ruined city to his station on the Pincian Hill. The bombardment was heavy that night—a night of deafening noise and bursts of frightening light, of maiming and of death. Somehow, Margaret and Ossoli survived it unharmed.

But the city did not. By the next day, the Romans knew they were defeated. There was no choice but to surrender to the French. The Roman government petitioned for terms. The French refused to grant any—the surrender must be unconditional. The French would not even guarantee safe conduct to Garibaldi, whose volunteer troops, fighting wherever in Italy the republican cause needed them, had played a magnificent part in the defense of the city. So Garibaldi's legion, now swelled by volunteers from other regiments, marched out of Rome, to continue the fight for independence in another part of Italy. In a dispatch to the *Tribune*, Margaret described their departure.

> Towards the evening of Monday, the 2nd of July, it was known that the French were preparing to cross the river and take possession of all the city. I went into the Corso with some friends; it was filled with citizens and military.

> The carriage was stopped by the crowd near the Doria Palace; the lancers of Garibaldi galloped along in full career. I longed for Sir Walter Scott to be on earth again and see them; all are light, athletic, resolute figures, many of the forms of the finest manly beauty of the South, all sparkling with its genius and ennobled by the resolute spirit, ready to dare, to do, to die. We followed them to the piazza of St. John Lateran. Never have I seen a sight so beautiful, so romantic, and so sad. . . . They had all put on the beautiful dress of the Garibaldi legion, the tunic of bright red cloth, the Greek cap, or else round hat with puritan plume. Their long hair was blown back from resolute faces; all looked full of courage. . . . I saw the wounded, all that could go, laden upon their baggage cars; some were already pale and fainting, still they wished to go. . . . The women were ready; their eyes too were resolved if sad. The wife of Garibaldi followed him on horseback. He himself was distinguished by the white tunic; his look was entirely that of a hero of the Middle Ages—his face still young, for the excitements of his life, though so many, have all been youthful and there is no fatigue upon his brow or cheek. . . . He went upon the parapet and looked upon the road with a spyglass, and, no obstruction being in sight, he turned his face for a moment back upon Rome, then led the way through the gate.

On July 4, 1849, the birthday of Margaret's country, the French troops entered Rome. The Roman Republic was dead.

17

Florentine Interlude

On July 10, Margaret wrote her final dispatch for the *Tribune*, a lament for the waste and ugliness of war.

> Yesterday I went over the scene of conflict. It was fearful even to *see* the Casinos Quattro Venti and Vascello, where the French and Romans had been several days so near one another, all shattered to pieces, with fragments of rich stucco and painting still sticking to rafters between the great holes made by the cannonade, and think that men had stayed and fought in them when only a mass of ruins. . . . A *contadino* showed me where thirty-seven braves are buried beneath a heap of wall that fell upon them in the shock of one cannonade. A marble nymph, with broken arm, looked sadly

> that way from her sun-dried fountain, some roses were blooming still, some red oleanders, amid the ruin. . . . I then entered the French ground, all mapped and hollowed like a honeycomb. A pair of skeleton legs protruded from a bank of one barricade; lower, a dog had scratched away its light covering of earth from the body of a man, and discovered it lying face upward all dressed; the dog stood gazing on it with an air of stupid amazement.

And she ended with an impassioned plea to her countrymen. The cause of freedom was, for the moment, dead in Italy. But to the north and east, another republic was alive, resisting the forces of foreign invasion. Hungary had been fighting for its independence for more than a year and in April the Hungarian Republic had been declared, with Lajos Kossuth as its president. Now that republic was under attack by two armies—the Russians from the north and the Austrians from the west. Surely, the American people would show their support for Hungary.

> Friends, countrymen, and lovers of virtue, lovers of freedom, lovers of truth! Be on the alert; rest not supine in your easier lives, but remember,
>
> "Mankind is one
> And beats with one great heart."

A few days after she wrote those words, Margaret and Ossoli packed their belongings and left Rome forever. Their departure had not been easy to arrange, but the city was not safe for either of them. The French were taking their revenge on the supporters of the revolution by repressions of all kinds, carting people off to prison on any flimsy pretext they could muster. At any moment, Margaret or Ossoli—or both of them—might be arrested.

They had no definite plans for the future. But one thing was clear: they wanted to be together. That meant they could no longer keep their relationship secret, and they no longer had any reason to remain separated from their child.

In these last months, they had heard virtually nothing about Angelino. With Rome under siege, communication with Rieti had become impossible. Margaret found her son's condition even worse than she had feared. His wet nurse's milk had failed. The baby had to be forced to take the wine and bread the nurse tried to feed him; the situation had been going on for weeks; he had been dreadfully ill; he was slowly starving to death. "He is worn to a skeleton," Margaret wrote Lewis Cass, "all his sweet childish graces fled; he is so weak that it seems to me he can scarcely ever revive to health."

For the next month, Angelino was her consuming concern. She and Ossoli watched over him every minute, concentrating the full force of their two lives onto saving his. It was a long struggle. But he gradually began to show signs of recovery, and by the time the month was over, they permitted themselves to believe that he would live. And now Margaret forced herself to face a task she had been dreading for more than a year. Since she could no longer keep Angelino and Ossoli a secret from her friends in Italy, she could no longer put off telling her mother about them. "A great pang of remorse came," she wrote to Caroline, "and I thought, if Angelino dies, I will not give her the pain of knowing that I have kept this secret from her. . . . When I found he would live, I wrote to her. It half-killed me."

Part of Margaret's distress sprang from her guilt at having kept the secret for so long. But by far the greatest part came from another source—the pain she knew she would bring her mother. The news, Margaret knew, would provide a field day for her enemies, and their behavior would inevitably hurt Mrs. Fuller. It was, after all, a scandal. A minor scandal, but a scandal nevertheless. All the people—and there were many—who resented and disliked Margaret would take delight in any tittering gossip they could launch against her. Even if she described herself as married, the very fact that she had kept Angelino's birth and her relationship with Ossoli a secret for so long would encourage them to put the ugliest possible construction on it. Mrs. Fuller would have to bear the brunt of all the cheap talk Margaret's news might give rise to in her own country.

Nevertheless, she had to be told. Margaret introduced the subject gently, after the general news.

> This brings me to the main object of my present letter, a piece of intelligence about myself which I had hoped I might be able to communicate to you in such a way as to give you pleasure. That

I cannot—after suffering much in silence with that hope—is like the rest of my earthly destiny.

The first moment, it may cause you a pang to know that your oldest child might long ago have been addressed by another name than yours, and has a little son a year old.

But, beloved mother, do not feel this long. I do assure you, that it was only great love for you that kept me silent. I have abstained a hundred times, when your sympathy, your counsel, would have been most precious, from a wish not to harass you with anxiety. Even now I would abstain, but it has become necessary on account of the child for us to live publicly and permanently together; and we have no hope in the present state of Italian affairs, that we can do it at any better advantage, for several years, than now.

My husband is a Roman, of a noble but impoverished house. His mother died when he was an infant, his father is dead since we met, leaving some property but encumbered with debts, in the present state of Rome hardly available, except by living there. . . . He is not in any respect such a person as people in general would expect to find with me. He had no instructor except an old priest, who entirely neglected his education; and of that which is contained in books he is absolutely ignorant. . . . On the other hand, he has excellent practical sense; has been a judicious observer of all that passed before his eyes; has a nice sense of duty . . . a very sweet temper, and great native refinement. His love for me has been unswerving and most tender. I have never suffered a pain that he could relieve.

> His devotion when I am ill is only to be compared with yours. . . . In him I have found a home, and one that interferes with no tie. Amid many ills and cares we have had much joy together in the sympathy with natural beauty, with our child, with all that is innocent and sweet.
>
> I do not know whether he will always love me so well, for I am the elder, and the difference will become, in a few years, more perceptible than now. But life is so uncertain, and it is so necessary to take good things with their limitations, that I have not thought it worthwhile to calculate too curiously. . . .
>
> What shall I say of my child? All might seem hyperbole, even to my dearest mother. In him I find satisfaction for the first time to the deep wants of my heart. He is a fair child, with blue eyes and light hair; very affectionate, graceful, and sportive. He was baptized in the Roman Catholic Church by the name of Angelo Eugene Philip, for his father, grandfather, and my brother. He inherits the title of Marquis.
>
> Write the name of my child in your bible, ANGELO OSSOLI, *born September 5, 1848*. God grant he may live to see you, and may prove worthy of your love!

With Angelino on the mend, Margaret and Ossoli were able to turn their thoughts to the future. It seemed to Margaret that it would be as difficult as the past had been. The United States was probably their best hope: it was where Margaret could most easily earn a living. But Angelino was not yet well enough for the trip, and they had practically no money. Ossoli went back to Rome to see if his family would buy back the few pieces of property his father had left him in his will. But the property, devastated by the war, was practically worthless, and his brothers were unwilling to help him in any way. They could not forgive him for having supported the revolution; the oldest, Giuseppe, refused even to see him.

So their last tie with the city was broken. There was nothing any longer to keep them in a part of Italy so full of sorry associations for both of them. Florence seemed the best place. Although it was occupied by the Austrians, they knew they would be safe. There was an English-speaking colony in Florence and among its members were two American couples—the Greenoughs and the Moziers—whom Margaret already knew. Elizabeth Barrett Browning and her husband, Robert Browning, were in Florence also. Margaret had hoped to meet them when she was in London—that scant three years ago that seemed another lifetime—but they had been out of town.

Margaret, Ossoli, and the baby did not go to Florence directly. They stopped for a few weeks at Perugia to rest, to be together in quiet, to gather their courage for the ordeal that might be ahead. While they were there, Margaret wrote a letter to Carlyle, requesting his help on the project that was dearest to her: the history she was writing of the Roman Revolution. If Carlyle could arrange to have it published in England, it would provide her and Ossoli with some much needed cash.

It was the end of September when the Ossolis arrived in Florence. Margaret's friends were cordial and welcoming. Even so, tongues began to wag. Elizabeth Barrett Browning wrote about it to a friend.

> The American authoress, Miss Fuller, has taken us by surprise at Florence, retiring from the Roman world with a husband and child above a year old. Nobody had even suspected a word of this underplot, and her American friends stood in mute astonishment before this apparition of them here. The husband is a Roman marquis appearing amiable and gentlemanly and having fought well, they say, at the siege, but with no pretensions to cope with his wife on any ground appertaining to the intellect.

Margaret would not even deign to notice the gossip. She wrote Emelyn Story, who, with her husband, was living temporarily in Venice:

> Thus far, my friends have received news that must have been an unpleasant surprise to them, in a way that, *a moi*, does them great honor. None have shown littleness or displeasure, at wanting my confidence while they were giving me their own. Many have expressed the warmest sympathy, and only one has a disposition to transgress the limit I myself had marked and to ask questions. With her, I think, it was because she was annoyed by things people said, and wanted to be able to answer them. I replied to her, that I had communicated already all I intended, and should not go into details as to the past—that when unkind things were said about me, she should let them pass. Will you,

> dear Emelyn, do the same? I am sure your affection for me will prompt you to add, that you feel confident whatever I have done has been in a good spirit, and not contrary to *my* ideas of right. For the rest, you will not admit for me—as I do not for myself—the rights of the social inquisition of the United States to know all the details of my affairs. If my mother is content, if Ossoli and I are content; if our child, when grown up, shall be content, that is enough. You and I know enough of the United States to be sure, that many persons there will blame whatever is peculiar. The lower minded persons, everywhere, are sure to think that whatever is mysterious must be bad. But I think there will remain for me a sufficient number of friends to keep my heart warm and to help me earn my bread; that is all that is of any consequence. Ossoli seems to me more lovely and good every day; our darling child is well now, and every day more gay and playful. . . .

That darling child was a constant revelation to Margaret. She wrote about him glowingly to her mother, her sister, her brothers, her friends. Right after Christmas, she sent this effusion to Caroline:

> He is now come to quite a knowing age (fifteen months). In the morning, as soon as dressed, he signs to come into our room; then draws our curtain, kisses me rather violently, pats my face, stretches himself and says *bravo*. Then expects as a reward to be tied in his chair and have his playthings. These engage him busily,

but still he calls us to sing and drum to enliven the scene. Sometimes he calls me to kiss his hand; he laughs very much at this. . . . Then I wash and dress him; that is his great time. He makes it last as long as he can, insisting to dress and wash me the while, kicking, throwing water about, full of all manner of tricks that I think girls never dream of. . . .

I feel so refreshed by his young life. Ossoli diffuses such a power and sweetness over every day that I cannot endure to think yet of our future. Too much have we suffered already trying to command it. I do not feel forced to make any effort yet. . . . Now for two months we have been tranquil; we have resolved to repose and enjoy being together as much as we can in this brief interval—perhaps all we shall ever know of peace. . . .

Christmas day I was just up, and Nino all naked on his sofa, when came some beautiful large toys that had been sent him: a bird, a horse, a cat that could be moved to express different things. It almost made me cry to see the kind of fearful rapture with which he regarded them—legs and arms extended, fingers and toes quivering, mouth made up to a little round O, eyes dilated. For a long time he did not even wish to touch them. After he began to, he was different with all the three: loving the bird; very wild and shouting with the horse; with the cat, putting her face close to his, staring in her eyes, and then throwing her away. . . . You would laugh to know how much remorse I feel that I never gave children more toys in the course of my life. I regret all the money I ever

> spent on myself or in little presents for grown people, hardened sinners. I did not know what pure delight could be bestowed. . . .

Margaret basked in the pure delight Angelino and Ossoli gave her for as long as she could.

18
Flight

The months of peace and happiness did not continue much longer. Both Margaret's and Ossoli's money was beginning to run out, and to bring in a little cash, Margaret undertook to tutor the Mozier's daughter, Isabella. She had been unable to reestablish her connection with the *Tribune*—probably because of the gossip in the United States about her. Word came from Carlyle that no English publisher would undertake to handle her book when it was finished. There were problems about copyrighting the work of a foreign author, and besides, Margaret's sympathy for the revolution was not widely shared in Britain, and she herself was under attack for her personal and political activities. Ossoli's position was no better. The Austrian authorities, having discovered that he had fought for the Roman Republic, began harassing him, and it was only through the intervention of American officials that he was finally left alone. Every day, the news from Rome grew more depressing, reaching its climax in April, just three years after Margaret and Ossoli had first met: the Pope reentered the city in triumph, as the head of its government.

That sealed their future. Ossoli could not return to Rome; Margaret could not earn a living in Italy. Despite Margaret's nagging fears of her reception in her country and Ossoli's reluctance to leave his native land, they had to go to America—only there could they and their son find any kind of peace.

But even after they made the decision, they remained reluctant to take the necessary steps. They did not have enough money for their passage; they would have to borrow it, and both of them felt ashamed. Nor was that the final hurdle. Ossoli had been warned by a fortune-teller when he was a child to beware the sea, and he could not shake off his forebodings. And Margaret had feared the ocean ever since her trip across the Atlantic with the Springs, four years before. The newspapers added to their anxieties. Almost daily, another story appeared about the wreck of some transatlantic steamer or packet—first the *Argo*, then the *Royal Adelaide*, then the *John Skeddy*. She and Ossoli had, for a while, talked of traveling on the *Argo*.

But they could not afford to keep on delaying, and when the Moziers introduced Margaret to Seth Hasty and his wife, Catherine, Margaret made up her mind. They were a pleasant couple, and she liked and trusted them. And Seth Hasty was Captain Hasty, in charge of the three-masted American merchantman the *Elizabeth*, which was scheduled to sail from Leghorn on May 17, with a cargo of almonds, oil, Carrara marble, and a huge statue of John C. Calhoun that had been sculpted by Hiram Powers, one of the American artists living in Italy. Only one passenger was so far scheduled to sail on the *Elizabeth*—a young Italian girl named Celeste Paolini, a domestic servant on her way to New York, where she had a job. After Margaret and Ossoli traveled up to Livorno to inspect the *Elizabeth*, which was taking on its cargo there, they added their names to the passenger list. Horace Sumner, the youngest brother of Charles Sumner, who had been a friend of Margaret's father, decided to sail with them. Horace, who was considerably younger than Margaret, had known and admired her since the days of Brook Farm, and when she and Ossoli arrived in Florence, where he was living, he had immediately looked them up. He was a boon to Ossoli: they were about the same age, and since his Italian was just about as bad as Ossoli's English, they exchanged language lessons.

Still, Margaret's forebodings continued. "I am suffering as never before the horrors of indecision," she wrote to a friend. ". . . Now that I am on the point of deciding to come in [the *Elizabeth*] people daily dissuade me, saying that I have no conception of what a voyage of sixty or seventy days will be in point of fatigue and suffering; that the cabin, being on deck, will be terribly exposed in case of a gale, etc., etc."

But the passage on the *Elizabeth* was cheaper than

any other they could arrange. And there were special advantages for all of them. Captain Hasty agreed to carry a goat aboard ship to provide milk for Angelino, and since Celeste had consented to act as nurse for the baby on the voyage, Margaret would be able to give her allotted daily time of work to the history. So the arrangement was concluded.

The first few days at sea were calm and relatively uneventful. The water was smooth, the weather beautiful. On the second day, Margaret and Angelino both got seasick, but they quickly recovered, and from that moment, Angelino became the ship's mascot—the pet of both the captain and the crew. They played with him; sang to him; walked him around while he took rides on his nanny goat. On the sixth day, May 23, Margaret celebrated her fortieth birthday. Everything was going smoothly. They began to relax.

Then, on the eighth day, Captain Hasty fell ill, and with each day that passed, he became sicker. His suffering was terrible to see. Ten days later, just as the ship had dropped anchor off Gibraltar, he died. Margaret described the burial at sea in a letter to Marcus and Rebecca Spring:

> . . . [He] was buried in deep water, the American Consul's barge towing out one from the ship which bore the body. It was Sunday and divinely calm. You cannot think how beautiful the whole thing was, the decent array and sad reverence of the sailors; the many ships with the banners flying; the stern pillars of Hercules bathed in

> roseate vapor; the little white sails diving into the blue depths with that solemn spoil of the good man, when he had been so agonized and gasping. . . .

The ship was held in quarantine at Gibraltar; when no further illness developed, it was permitted to sail again—this time under the command of the first mate, Mr. Bangs, a man far less experienced in the ways of the sea than Captain Hasty.

But it was not his inexperience that worried Margaret. Two days after the ship was allowed to set sail, Angelino came down with the same illness that had killed the captain—apparently smallpox. For nine days the boy seemed on the verge of death; then he began to recover. The vaccine he had been given in Rieti was evidently not potent enough to immunize him completely, but it had at least reduced the intensity of the illness.

With Angelino recovered, Margaret and Ossoli tried to settle into enjoying the voyage. Ossoli and Horace Sumner exchanged language lessons. Margaret worked on her history and spent much time with the captain's widow, in an effort to console her. Angelino rode triumphantly up and down the deck on his nanny goat's back. But the journey seemed endless. They had left Gibraltar on June 9; by the second week in July, they were still on the high seas.

Finally, the American coastline came into sight, and on July 18 the *Elizabeth* was off the Jersey shore. Mr. Bangs assured his passengers that they would be in New York by early the next morning, and he suggested that they begin to pack their trunks. A wave of relief swept through Margaret as she checked through Angelino's clothing, selecting the outfit he would wear.

But during the night, a sharp wind arose—a wind almost of gale force. Mr. Bangs close-reefed his sails and, sure that he had his bearings right, continued the ship on its course.

It was four in the morning when the disaster occurred. Mr. Bangs had miscalculated, and traveled too far east, and the *Elizabeth* struck a sandbar off Fire Island. The force of the impact and the weight of the marble in the hold broke the ship's bottom; she began to list desperately, and the waves swept over her. The lifeboats were torn loose and carried off by the seething sea. The passengers and crew were separated from one another—the crew in the forecastle, the passengers aft, in the cabin. Somehow, Margaret and Ossoli remained calm. She comforted Angelino, who was wailing in terror; he prayed with Celeste, who had become hysterical.

By the next morning, the crew had found the passengers, and led them to the forecastle—a sailor carrying Angelino in a canvas bag slung around his neck. The Fire Island shore was clearly visible, only a few hundred yards away. At about nine, the gale subsided for a while and Horace Sumner and two of the sailors jumped overboard, to try to swim to shore and find help. The sailors made it, Horace did not—his body disappeared beneath the foam. Figures appeared on the beach and for a short while everyone felt hope. But it soon became evident that these were beach pirates, interested only in the cargo from the *Elizabeth*'s hold that had been thrown up on the shore.

The hours passed, and still help did not come. The second mate, Mr. Davis, proposed a scheme: each of the passengers would lie, facedown, on a plank from the boat; a sailor would be lashed behind it, and would swim the plank and its passenger to safety. Mrs. Hasty agreed to take the chance, and Margaret and Ossoli watched as one of the sailors swam her safely to shore.

But Margaret refused to travel this route to safety. She would not be parted from Ossoli or Angelino. And she persisted in her refusal, insisting that help would soon come from the shore. Nor would she change her mind even when, at noon, Mr. Bangs gave orders to abandon ship. There was a lull in the storm then; he knew they must take advantage of it, that the poor wreck could not withstand another gust of wind or another surge of sea.

But he could say nothing to move Margaret. Finally, he gave the order, "Save yourselves," and he and all the rest of the crew except the steward and three sailors jumped overboard. By three in the afternoon the gale was still raging and the ship had begun to break up completely. The crewmen pleaded with Margaret; again she refused to leave. Finally, one of the sailors snatched Angelino into his arms, promising that he would save the child or die. Just at that moment, a mountain of rushing water struck the ship, and the foremast fell, ripping through the deck and flinging everyone on board into the water.

Twenty minutes later, the bodies of Angelino and the sailor who was carrying him were washed ashore, still warm. Margaret, Ossoli, and their baby's nurse vanished. Their bodies were never found.

Epilogue

Margaret's death shocked everyone who knew her. The survivors' story of the wreck must have told them that she and her family might also have reached safety, had that been what she wished. Some of them came close to acknowledging it. Elizabeth Barrett Browning, who had become very fond of Margaret during the time the Ossolis were in Florence, wrote to a friend: "Was she happy in anything, I wonder? She told me that she never was. May God have made her happy in her death."

Emerson was stricken. But his even-keeled optimism would not permit him to entertain the thought that Margaret's death could have been self-willed. He had always been uncomfortable with the dark, "unhealthy" side of her nature, and he could not bring himself to believe how far it might have driven her. The storm was to blame and the reef off Fire Island; it was not she. "On Friday, July 19," he wrote in his journal, "Margaret dies on rocks of Fire Island Beach within sight of and within sixty rods of the shore. To the last her country proves inhospitable to her; brave, eloquent, subtle, accomplished, devoted, constant soul!"

She required a tribute, Emerson knew, and before the month was out he, William Henry Channing, and Sam Ward agreed to write a memorial of her, drawing not only on their recollections and the recollections of others who had known her, but on the journals she had left in her mother's care before she went to New York. All the materials she had brought with her from Italy—not only her later journals, but her history of the Roman Revolution—were lost in the shipwreck. As soon as he heard the news of Margaret's death, Henry Thoreau had rushed down to Fire Island to try at least to recover the Ossolis' possessions, but all of them had been swallowed by the churning sea.

Somehow or other, Sam Ward dropped out of the collaboration. Apparently, he was no better able to deal with the demands of Margaret's character when she was dead than he had been when she was alive. His place was taken by one of her oldest friends, James Freeman Clarke, who helped her make her first break with Boston and with ivory tower Transcendentalism. Mazzini and the Brownings promised to write pieces on Margaret's years in Italy. But although they kept their promises, the pieces never arrived. Possibly the censors destroyed them, since they dealt with the revolution in Rome.

In their zeal to do Margaret justice, Margaret's biographers went through her journals with scissors as well as pencils, not only correcting her punctuation and her grammar, which were often erratic, but also destroying whole sections of what she had written. Some of her words, after all, might not bring credit to her: perhaps they were harsh—on others and on herself. There had been enough criticism of Margaret during her lifetime; now that she was dead, they wanted to lay it to rest. As a result, the Margaret they painted was almost too good to be true. Yet even her enemies accepted this less than frank picture. The tragedy of her death and the obscenity that had surrounded it—the scavengers on the shore who, in a day and a half, had made no effort to bring help to the stricken ship—made people eager to see Margaret as a heroine. It consoled them for the ugly things that had been said about her when she was alive.

But in 1852, the same year the *Memoirs* appeared, another view of Margaret was presented that was far less flattering. In that year Hawthorne, by now famous, published his novel, *The Blithedale Romance.* Its setting was obviously Brook Farm; Zenobia, its arrogant leading lady—one could hardly call her a heroine—was obviously based on Margaret. Zenobia was brilliant, dramatic, and cold; a woman whose character did not entitle her to the admiration and fame she somehow had; a woman who was, indeed, unlovable, who suffered from the tragic deficit Margaret felt in herself. At the close of the book, Zenobia drowns herself because the man she loves has chosen a woman closer to Hawthorne's ideal: a simple, quiet girl, with only sweetness and selflessness to recommend her.

The pro- and anti-Margaret factions raged for years, and even after his death, Hawthorne contributed to fanning the fires against her. In the second edition of his *Italian Journals*, prepared by his son, passages about Margaret were included that had been omitted from the first—he described her as "a great humbug" with a "strong, heavy, unpliable, and, in many respects, defective and evil nature," and reported that the Moziers, the American friends in Florence who had helped Margaret book her fatal passage home, called Ossoli stupid beyond belief, unable to tell the difference between a thumb and a big toe.

But by the end of the century, Margaret had faded into unimportance, leaving unanswered a multitude of questions—questions she herself may possibly have answered in her own words. We will never have her history of the Roman Revolution. Would it have established her as a major literary figure? Was it the magnum opus that would have made it impossible to relegate her to obscurity? We will never know the intimate secrets her friends excised from her journals. Would these have helped us better understand her complex character? Would they have explained her moods, her fears, the extraordinary impact—whether positive or negative—she had on everyone who knew her? We will never even know whether or not she and Ossoli were actually married. Among the vanished papers was the packet she had given Emelyn Story during the siege of Rome. Emelyn never opened it, and she returned it to Margaret when she, Ossoli, and Angelino were living in Florence. It is doubtful that the packet contained a marriage certificate. But somewhere among her other papers there may have been one, dated sometime in 1850, the year she died. A little more than a year thereafter, Ossoli's sister wrote to Ellen Channing, Margaret's sister, that her brother had told her he and Margaret were married in Florence.

But with all the mysteries she left behind her, the most important things about Margaret and her life are entirely clear. She was a woman of extraordinary courage, conviction, and character, who never gave up the struggle for what she believed in and whose deepest belief was in the need to make a better world.

Selected Bibliography

The books below provided the information on which this one was based. I can add only one small fact, which corrects what seems to be a common misapprehension among Margaret Fuller's later biographers: that the Sam Ward of whom she was so fond was Sam Ward of New York, a clever adventurer and a minor scoundrel, who made and lost several fortunes while he was still young and who finally wound up in Washington, D.C., where he acted so effectively as a representative of big business interests that he was known as the King of the Lobby. Margaret's Sam Ward was Samuel Gray Ward, a distant cousin of the adventurer and a Bostonian, who had no such dubious distinctions as his New York relative. Aside from the similarity in their names, there is another good reason for the misapprehension. The New York Sam Ward had a sister, Julia, who married Samuel

Gridley Howe of Boston, who became famous for writing the words to "The Battle Hymn of the Republic," and who was among Margaret's warmest admirers, both during her lifetime and after her death.

BIOGRAPHIES

ANTHONY, KATHERINE. *Margaret Fuller, A Psychological Biography.* New York: Harcourt, Brace & Co., 1921.

BELL, MARGARET. *Margaret Fuller.* Introduction by Mrs. Franklin D. Roosevelt. New York: C. Boni, 1930.

BROWN, ARTHUR W. *Margaret Fuller.* New York: Twayne Publishers, 1964.

DEISS, JOSEPH JAY. *The Roman Years of Margaret Fuller.* New York: Thomas Y. Crowell Co., 1969.

EMERSON, R. W.; CHANNING, W. H.; and CLARKE, J. F. *Memoirs of Margaret Fuller Ossoli.* 2 vols. Boston: Phillips, Sampson & Co., 1852.

HIGGINS, THOMAS WENTWORTH. *Margaret Fuller Ossoli.* Boston: Houghton, Mifflin & Co., 1884.

ROSTENBERG, LEONA. "Margaret Fuller's Roman Diary." *Journal of Modern History,* vol. 12, June 2, 1940.

STERN, MADELINE B. *The Life of Margaret Fuller.* New York: E. P. Dutton & Co., Inc., 1942.

WADE, MASON. *Margaret Fuller: Whetstone of Genius.* New York: The Viking Press, 1940.

WORKS BY MARGARET FULLER

FULLER, MARGARET. *Love-Letters of Margaret Fuller.* Introduction by Julia Ward Howe. New York: AMS Press, Inc., 1970.

———. *Woman in the Nineteenth Century.* New York: W. W. Norton & Co., Inc., 1971.

MILLER, PERRY, ed. *Margaret Fuller, American Romantic: A Selection from Her Writings and Correspondence.* Ithaca, N.Y.: Cornell University Press, 1970.

WADE, MASON, ed. *The Writings of Margaret Fuller.* Clifton, N.J.: Augustus M. Kelly, 1973. Includes *Summer on the Lakes.*

BACKGROUND READING

BOLLER, PAUL F., JR. *American Transcendentalism, 1830–1860.* New York: G. P. Putnam's Sons, 1974.

BROOKS, VAN WYCK. *The Flowering of New England.* New York: E. P. Dutton & Co., Inc., 1952.

HAWTHORNE, NATHANIEL. *The Blithedale Romance.* In *The Complete Novels and Selected Tales of Nathaniel Hawthorne*, edited by Norman Holmes Pearson. New York: The Modern Library, 1965.

MILLER, PERRY, ed. *The American Transcendentalists: Their Prose and Poetry.* New York: Doubleday Anchor Books, 1957.

———. *The Transcendentalists: An Anthology.* Cambridge, Mass.: Harvard University Press, 1971.

SAMS, HENRY W., ed. *Autobiography of Brook Farm: A Book of Primary Source Material.* Englewood Cliffs, N.J.: Prentice-Hall, Inc., 1958.

SHEPARD, ODELL. *Pedlar's Progress: The Life of Bronson Alcott.* Boston: Little, Brown & Co., 1937.

THARP, LOUISE HALL. *The Peabody Sisters of Salem.* Boston, Little, Brown & Co., 1950.

———. *Three Saints and a Sinner (Julia Ward Howe,*

Louisa, Annie, and Sam Ward). Boston: Little, Brown & Co., 1956.

VAN DOREN, MARK. *Nathaniel Hawthorne*. New York: William Sloane Associates, Inc., 1949.

Index

Wallingford Public Library
Wallingford, CT 06492
A2170 098290 6